SO THAT OTHERS MIGHT LIVE
(THE SOCIOLOGY OF SAR)

SEARCH AND RESCUE IN THE RED RIVER GORGE

BY DON F. FIG

So That Others Might Live (The Sociology of SAR)
Search and Rescue In The Red River Gorge
By Don Fig

Printed On-Demand

First published in 2007 by Publishing Services, Inc.,
3750 Priority Way South Drive, Suite 114
www.wordclay.com

Softcover ISBN 978-1-64338-301-9

24 HOUR Books
On-Demand Publishing

24 Hours Books, Inc.
14 S. Queen Street, Mt. Sterling, Kentucky 40353, USA
www.reformationpublishers.com
Email rpublisher@aol.com
Orders 1-800-765-2464
Information 859-520-3757
Text 606-359-2064
Fax 859-520-3357

Printed and bound in the United States of America

DON FIG & THE RED RIVER GORGE

You can't talk about the modern history of the Red River Gorge without talking about Don Fig. For five decades, Don was the voice, hand and conscience of the USFS in Kentucky's land of federal designations. From the creation of the Clifty Wilderness, the special geological and archaeological areas and the designation of the Red as a wild and scenic river, Don was there to guide and shepherd this section of the Daniel Boone National Forest into the special place it is today. His passing in April of 2020 marked the end of an era and the Gorge as well as the world at large are diminished without him.

It is with a sense of indebtedness and responsibility to Don's legacy that Friends of Red River Gorge has undertaken the task of bringing Don's books about the Red River Gorge back into print. We do this so that a new generation can share in the knowledge, wit and wisdom of a man whose memory deserves to be preserved along with the land he so loved.

Dave McCreary, Executive Director
Friends of Red River Gorge
Jan 2021

Proceeds from the sale of this book support our nonprofit volunteer efforts. A portion will go to the Fig Fund benefiting local search and rescue teams and others keeping Don's legacy of service alive.

Friends of Red River Gorge
271 West Main St. Ste. 408
Lexington, KY 40507

FOREWORD

The Red River Gorge, an area nestled in the foothills of the Appalachian Mountains of Kentucky has countless miles of sandstone cliffs, deep gorges, rugged trails and towering arches, visitors often find themselves in trouble and sometimes worse. Don and his team of Volunteers, conducted rescue operations for over 45 years and racked up an impressive number of responses exceeding 1600. This number is even more impressive when you factor that much of this was accomplished before cell phones, GPS and other tracking/mapping devices were readily available for both rescuers and the general public. Don Fig has been and will continue to be a legend when it comes to rescues in the wilds of the Red River Gorge.

Although some things have changed over the years, much of what was used in those early days has remained the same. Utilizing rope systems to gain access to individuals below cliff lines is often the safest and most efficient technique that is still being utilized even today.

I can still remember the first time I had a conversation with Don Fig about Search & Rescue. It was around 2004 and my own career in Search & Rescue in the Red River Gorge was in its infancy. He was setting at his desk in the basement of the Gladie Center. A place he had called home for over 50 years. Don was dressed in his usual USFS uniform and every bit looking the part. He was older then but I still remember thinking how strong this man looks. His arms were muscular and he looked like he could wrestle a bear.

As Don's retirement was approaching, a passing of the torch from rescues being conducted by the USFS to the local Search & Rescue teams was underway. Local Volunteers not only had to be sourced but trained. It was a daunting task of sorts, one that would take several years to complete.

Volunteers of Search & Rescue share a lot of common traits; a desire to help others, passion for the outdoors, being part of a team and a bit of an adrenalin junkie, all rolled into one. The teams were green back in 2004 with little training and even less gear but the stage was set to carry Don's legacy forward and forward we marched.

Those first couple of years were a time of growth in knowledge, experience and confidence. Within the first six months of forming the Wolfe County Search & Rescue Team, we responded to our first fatality at Chimney Rock Overlook, it would not be our last. It was a sobering reminder that what we do is serious business, it's dangerous and lives will be impacted, not only for those we rescue/recover but our own as well. As the popularity of the Red has grown over the years so has SAR responses. Fifty or more rescues in a year isn't unheard of these days. Don always kept tabs on us and once dropped me a message. It was short and to the point; "I'm watching the amazing work your team is doing and I'm proud of you." Rest easy my friend, we will take it from here.

"So that Others Might Live"

—John May, Chief, Wolfe County Search & Rescue

ABOUT DON F. FIG

The author is a long-term employee of the U.S. Forest Service stationed in the Red River Gorge for over 45 years. He has actively performed well over 1600 Search and Rescue missions and has received many national and local awards including:

USDA Honor Award
Presidential Citation
Congressman's Award of Merit
Congressional Record
Ky Senate Award for Dedicated and Meritorious Service
Outstanding Performance in Leadership
Outstanding Performance in SAR
Heroism and Dedication

He is a published author of books and articles including:

- **TALES OF THE RED RIVER GORGE**
- **A HISTORY OF THE FITCHBURG FURNACE**
- **THE SOCIOLOGY OF SEARCH AND RESCUE**
- **FROM ROCKSHELTER TO GUNBARREL**
- **AN INCIPIENT INDUSTRY OF THE RED RIVER GORGE**

FRONTISPIECE

The frontispiece was created by Dan Dourson and represents an enigmatic natural arch as a background with an apparition of an owl superimposed over the rugged silhouette of the rock. The arch symbolizes strength of character and resoluteness, while the owl portrays wisdom and vigilance in watching over the Red River Gorge.

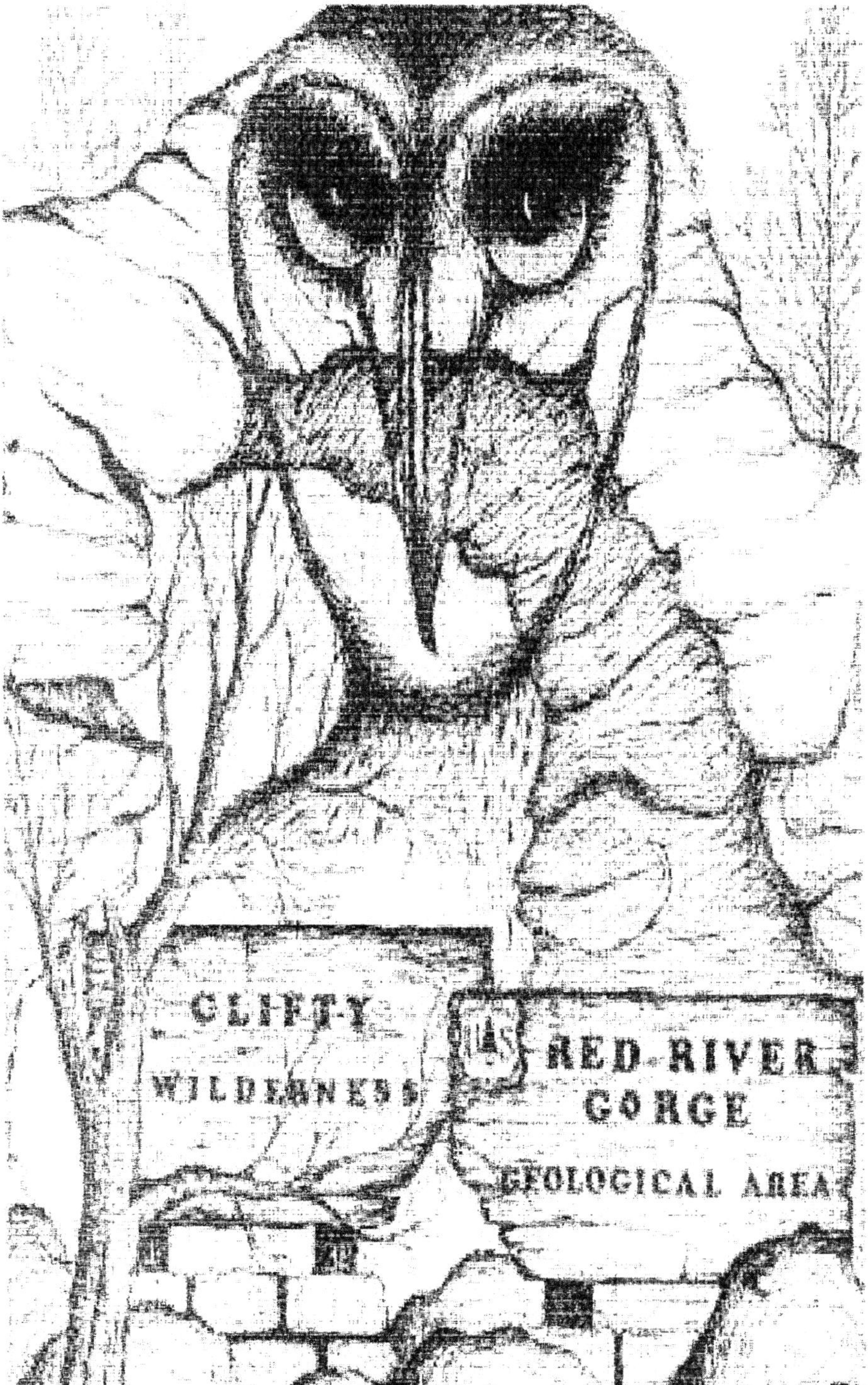
CLIFTY
WILDERNESS
RED RIVER
GORGE
GEOLOGICAL AREA

THE BAH KUA

A Chinese philosopher, Lao Tzu and his Taoism brought forth the belief that all life is either Yang or Yin, good or bad, positive or negative and so forth. The concept is as circle with a line similar to the letter S shading half of it. The small end of Yang slips into the large part of Yin, which at the same time, slides its small end in the large part of Yang. Imperceptibly, each changes the other all in a circle of completeness. This design is known as the Bah Kua and represents the balance between good and evil and all the other opposites. Everyone lives according to his nature, his bad shades into his good and vice versa. The light half represents the Yang force and the dark half denotes Yin.

As a comparison with Confucianism which sought the full development of humans through moral education and the establishment of an orderly hierarchical society, Taoism (pronounced dow-ism) sought to preserve human life by following the Way of Nature (Tao) and by reverting to primitive agrarian communities and a government that did not control or interfere with life. Taoism attempted to bring the individual into perfect harmony with nature through a mystical union with the Tao, and through this union, the individual

could transcend nature and even life and death. During the 4th century BC, naturalism offered an analysis of the workings of the universe based upon certain principles: Yang and Yin, which represented the interacting dualities of nature, such as male and female, dark and light, and winter and summer.

In an analogous sense, this is similar to the spokes of a wheel The wheel rim is the circle which holds ideas, mites them with other ideas, sorts them out and feeds them back along a spoke, and that in turn shoots out a changed idea.

In a story the old philosopher, ChuangTzu, tells of a dream. In the dream he was a butterfly. When he awoke, he said he did not know if he was a man who dreamed he was a butterfly, or a butterfly who dreamed he was a man. The merging of concepts, not either-or, but both-and. In the Bah Kua there is no straight fine; the line bends back on itself, forming a perfect circle. Everything is relative.
Mohism, founded by Mo-tzu during the 5th century BC, taught strict utilitarianism and mutual love among all people regardless of family or social relationships.

Hsun-tzu teachings in legalism was the dominant philosophy during the 4th & 3rd centuries. The idea was that human nature was incorrigibly evil and that strict controls were needed to regulate human conduct, led to the legalist developing a political philosophy that emphasized strict laws and harsh punishment in the control of every aspect of human society. Enormous public work projects, such as the Great Wall, were accomplished with forced labor and at great cost in human life.

The Bah Kua symbol is utilized in some modern homes as the expectancy of a balancing out of contentious forces.

How is this concept applied to SAR? Rescue acts out a heroic myth of cheating death. Thus the Yang forces (good) may be applied to the rescuer while the Yin forces (bad) symbolize the accident. The union of these two opposite forces may represent the successful rescue.

THE CARNIGE AWARD

On July 27, 1996 a subject attempted a rappel from Grays Arch without gloves. He lost control on the descent and could not recover. Matt Gibson, who was underneath the arch, sized up the situation and tried to stop the subject's fall
by grabbing the rope. By this time the subject was too close and landed on Matt. This broke his fall and undoubtedly saved his life. Subject suffered severe burns on his hands, but was otherwise not injured. Matt was not so fortunate, suffering a broken collarbone and ribs. Matt later received the Carnige Award for his heroic act.

On November 10, 2005, the rescue was reenacted using the original participants where possible. The film will be aired nationally in 2006.

Matt was not a member of a rescue team, yet he acted quickly and decisively, risking his own life "So That Others Might Live".

GRAYS ARCH

THE RED RIVER GORGE EXPERIENCE

"Let me do it while I can. No delay, for it is plain
I shall not pass this way again."
-Anon-

What the Golden Fleece was to Jason and his Argonauts so is the enticement of the Red River Gorge to visitors of Kentucky. Down through the ages, the lure of this land where spiritual renewal may be had for the asking has intrigued visitors and local residents alike. Since the sheep is symbolic of innocence and gold represents supreme spirituality and glorification, the Golden Fleece signifies the quest of the Argonauts was for supreme strength of spirit through purity of soul -that quality which distinguished Sir Galahad, the mediaeval Knight of the Holy Grail. What quest brings the human element to the Gorge? Not unlike the days of Sir Galahad where many Knights vowed to search for the Holy Grail, the cup from which Christ drank at the Last Supper, there appears to be a resurrection of vows among visitors, seeking a regeneration of life through the transcendental of natural phenomenon.

Sadly, as people call for their "Golden spurs and richest mail", death and danger as in ancient times, lurk in the journey for the symbolic cup. Others seek in vain oftentimes the better part of their lives only to find that "The Grail in my castle here is found," as did Sir Launfal in the epic of the same name.

The quest for salvation is one of the fundamental principles of most religious traditions. Salvation reminds me of a story told by an old-time resident.

A young man in the Gorge area entered a church where the preacher was in an intense sermon. Noting the young man's entry, the preacher cried. "Young man. Are you looking for SALvation."? No! came the reply. "I'm looking for Sal Sargent."

Devil Sal, or the Devil Woman of Red River as she was widely known, was famous for her "tincture of lightfoot." In those days

the entire family helped with the food supply. One fine late summer day, Devil Sal and her two sons set out for the top of a cliff where blueberries grew in profusion. The route to the rim was a long narrow crack in the cliff. The children scrambled up easily, but Devil Sal being a robust woman, found the crack a tight fit. However, by maneuvering around and using small niches for hand and footholds, she finally managed to gain the top.

The view from this spiny prominence was superb, however her mind was not on the view. She had brought two large tin buckets and her immediate concern was filling these with blueberries and this was finally accomplished.

When it was time to start toward the valley below, Devil Sal let her children go down the crack first and they were soon safety down. She started to descend the narrow crack in the cliff and became wedged in a tight spot. Placing the tin buckets on her shoulders, she tried to squirm free but found herself in a position where she could neither go up or down. Her children, seeing her quandary, ran off and left her tightly jammed in the crack.

Devil Sal, after a period of time, managed to free herself. Needless to say, there was considerable activity when she finally reached home.

That is why the area was named Pinch-Em-Tight Gap a name it still bears today, while standing like a giant cenotaph to the memory of Devil Sal.

This illustrates that climbing cliffs in the Gorge is nothing new. It has been going on since the early 1900's the time period of Devil Sal. In those days cliff climbing was a matter of necessity, now it is for pleasure and spiritual renewal. Jewel Rock, a popular rock climbing area, was named for Blue Jewel, another local Gorge resident, because he climbed it so often to pick blueberries, and Pyramid Rock was climbed by Steve Dehart who, as the legend goes, placed two gold coins on the summit for anyone who could climb the rock. The coins have never been found

Apparently, falls from high cliffs were a rarity in the early days. I have found few documented or hearsay cases of death on the cliff faces. Were people more cautious in that day? Probably not. There

has been a monumental increase of visitors to the Gorge area since that time. As common sense dictates, the probability of accidents increase with the intensity of use.

By the early 1900's many of the more prominent rocks in the Gorge had been climbed by local residents at that time rather than recreational climbers. Climbing became a sport in this area sometime in the early 1960's and now the Red River Gorge Experience is a powerful beacon bringing climbers in from all over the nation and even foreign countries.

When I was a young climber in the early 60's seeking what is now called the "Red River Gorge Experience" my first ascent was Tower Rock and than on to Pyramid Rock in a quest for the legendary gold coins left by Steve Dehart atop this prominence. I did not find the coins but I was left with a new respect for Steve and the other early mountaineers who scaled these pinnacles without ropes or protection devices. I did not leave out Jewell Rock, but later learned Blue had constructed a rudiment- ladder in order to facilitate getting up and down.

Many rocks with resplendent names existed and I wanted to climb them all. Names like Courthouse, Haystack, Eagles Peak, Pinnacle, Smokestack, to name a few and all offering a challenging experience for a young man who was rapidly succumbing to the mystic of the natural phenomenon of rocks and arches, along with the unique and fascinating history.

I became captivated with the Big Eared Bat and White-Haired Goldenrod and was meticulous in recording all sites encountered with these species. At the same time, the rescues were increasing in complexity as more and more people strayed farther from the roads to find the hidden treasures of the Gorge. All these problems resulted in the development of the "Red River Gorge System," a unique blend of stretcher raise configurations, which were singular to the Gorge. As the rescues increased in difficult}', so did the technology expertise needed to perform such maneuvers. The team was more than equal to this challenge.

A problem was promotions, transfers and attrition of the team that sometime thinned the ranks considerably, leaving many "empty saddles in the old corral." To work as a unit, especially amid the

high cliffs of the Gorge, takes training, discipline and a desire to be of service. When a team member leaves for whatever reason, his presence is keenly missed and he must be replaced with a new face but old traditions.

While all this is a background to the Sociology of SAR, it is intended to give the reader a brief insight into the mystic fascination visitors have with the Red River Gorge.

INTRODUCTION

Writing about the Sociology of SAR is somewhat akin to Star Trek's "To boldly go where no man has gone before". Similar to Star Trek, we must navigate uncharted space to explore a new world in which we quickly pass from fact into a twilight zone of inference, in that we can say not, this is true, but only probably this is true. And from thence into a region of darkness, lit here and there, by a guess, speculation or theory. Not being a sociologist, or even remotely a reasonable facsimile thereof, I can only draw on the experience of over 1600 Search and Rescue missions to graph the way for this composition. Dialogue with hundreds of accident victims in the Red River Gorge has provided scant insight into the domain of trauma common to high cliff accidents. What of the rescuer himself? Where does he fit into the symbolic representation?

A few years ago one of the key members of the SAR team, seasoned by hundreds of missions, decided he had enough and was leaving the team. "Too much blood, pain and suffering," was his reason. In all my years of SAR, I have never seen his equal. In the chronicles of SAR, Johnny Faulkner's name indeed stands tall.

Recently, at a program I was presenting, a lady remarked that I must have been a lucky person to have survived all the missions. Perhaps she was right. I guess my "luck" has always been people. People like Jack Courtney, Gary Hawkins, Johnny Faulkner, and always Kendal Culbertson, a long time veteran of the team, and an outstanding paragon of the SAR profile.

The original members of the Red River Gorge Mountain Rescue Team are long gone, leaving many "empty saddles in the old corral." Transfers, promotions, and just plain wearing down took their toil changing the social relationship of the team. This change is in fact, altruism. Social patterns are constantly changing as is society as a whole. You can either change to meet the conditions of the new society or die with the old one. It is not really good-bye, but it is farewell. (A' Tout a' 1' Heure), a French phrase meaning, "I'll see you again." Some people cling to that hope.

An Old Testament Psalm puts it all in perspective:

"As for man, his days are as grass; as a flower of the field, so he flourisheth. For the wind passeth over it, and it is gone; and the place thereof shall know it no more."

And now, THE SOCIOLOGY OF SAR, as it appears from my viewpoint.

THE SOCIOLOGY OF SEARCH AND RESCUE

BY
DON F. FIG

PROLOGUE

"The most difficult thing in life is to know yourself"
-Thates-

I had always said my retirement date would be when Sky Bridge fell or I reached 1300 rescue missions. There is no significance in that number. It was just an unrealistic goal visualized by a young man just starting his career. I never dreamed of even remotely approaching such a total, and certainty did not conclude Sky Bridge would fall. It was simply the impression of someone new to the area and seeing Sky Bridge for the first time.

Rescue mission number 1300 occurred on May 14, 1995 near the edge of dark. I was just completing a rescue at nifty Creek, about 2 miles upstream on the Red River, when the call came that a rock climber was injured near Indian Creek. Intimidating clouds were banking in the west when I arrived in the area and learned the climber was about 1 mile from the roadway. As darkness would soon shroud the land, I hastened to the scene ahead of the rescue team and the equipment. On a mantle about 20 feet up. I located a young muscular male subject that had fallen about 50 feet while climbing. Carefully working my way up to him I pulled myself over the edge onto the shelf. A quick examination indicated a dislocated hip. Patient was conscious with good vital signs. By this time the rescue team had arrived along with full darkness and a brewing storm. The patient was gently as possible moved onto a backboard prior to placement in the stokes. A short simple lowering system sufficed to reach ground level. The wheel was attached to the litter and we set out to beat the approaching thunderhead. We did not succeed. About half way out the storm overtook us with a brutal fury. Headlamps were useless in the torrential downpour. We kept on moving, with the ground quickly becoming muddy and slick, causing the litter wheel to slip sideways on the slopes. Meanwhile, the patient never complained even

though the deluge was penetrating the covering I had placed over him. Finally we reached the roadway where the victim was loaded into the waiting ambulance.

The patient was very appreciative of the team effort and expressed his gratitude for the quick response and technical expertise.

The ambulance moved out in the driving rainstorm enroute to Clark County. The rescue team went their separate ways, leaving me to ponder my 1300th rescue mission in the darkness of a dying thunderstorm.

My 1300th rescue mission came and went and still I did not retire. Sky Bridge appears constant as ever. No, this is not really so. Over the years I have noted the column beneath the bridge shrinking from natural erosion, helped along by deep initials carved into the surface by thoughtless vandals. The old saying "Only the rocks live forever," is incorrect in this modern world.

The Sociology of Search and Rescue was something I have never really considered up to now. To me, SAR is a transportation problem of removing the victim from some precipitous cliff ledge to a place of safety and medical care. There are four core elements to any rescue: Locate Reach, Treat, and Evacuate. There is also a critical fifth element that really should come before the other four. It is Preventive Search and Rescue. PSAR will be examined elsewhere in this report.

That there should be close bonds between sociology and SAR is hardly surprising since unsafe acts or conditions commonly initiates a mission. The variety of social contact in dealing with the victim, rescuers, relatives and media is jarring. Add dog owners to this and you have a hodgepodge of social interactions.

Sometimes a dog owner can be difficult to understand in stress situations concerning their pet. They fail to comprehend the peril, especially in falls from cliffs, in which they place a rescuer. Not only the ordinary hazards, but dog bites as well.

Once a small dog fell about 20 feet to a ledge near Sky Bridge. The frenzied dog owner was wild with excitement that could not have been more had a child fallen. Loudly insisting that I retrieve her dog, the lady appeared on the brink of collapse. Obtaining my rappelling gear I set out to rescue the dog. When I reached the shelf, the dog became very hostile. I was in some uncertainty how to best handle this situation. I caught up the dog, receiving bites in the process, and tied his jaws together. Since there was no one on top to assist me, I placed the little Chihuahua Toodles by name, inside my jacket and started onward/upward. Almost to the top, the webbing over the jaws came loose and the chewing on my shirt began along with ominous growls and barks. "Don't you hurt my baby" came the grumble from above. Hurt her baby indeed! I was the one under attack. However her voice did have some affect on the dog. He stopped his viscous display of teeth and became relatively calm. As soon as I gained the cliff top, the lady grabbed Toodles and without a word of thanks or a single backward glance set off up the trail.

This was my first dog rescue. but it was certainly not to be my last. There was nothing left to do but step for home and bind my wounds.

MY BROTHER'S KEEPER

Fain would I climb, yet fear Ito fall
-Sir Walter Raleigh-

What is sociology? It is usually defined as the science or origin, development, and nature of problems confronting society. Search and Rescue, hereafter referred to as SAR, is ordinarily defined as helping another in need who cannot help themselves. Thus the Sociology of SAR might be considered for this composition as offering a better understanding of victim behavior under conditions of stress. Also included, are behavior patterns of SAR personnel and relatives of victim. This report is based on long-term observations and dialogues. It has no scientific basis, and makes no pretense as to accuracy.

Chimney Rock deserves a special mention. This location has been the scene of numerous accidents and death. It appears that climbing over the overlook safety rails and making an attempt to jump across a four foot crack to the chimney borders on the inane audacious. The chimney is a vertical crack in the face of a cliff, and has been the scene of my most difficult rescues. The calls reporting accidents in this area invariably strikes a chord of apprehension in me.

There have been so many incidents at Chimney rock, but two remain anamnesis. It was a fine summer night, much too rare to be thinking about injure• and death. Yet this very night would yield the death of a young man and an unusual rescue calling for exceptional measures. The call came while I was relaxing at home. Chimney Rock again! According to the information received, a young man had been jumping back and forth across the crack and plunged into the crevice.

Darkness had shrouded the land, as I made preparations for the rescue plan. I was fortunate tonight as I had my best team members with me. Kendal Culbertson and Butch Till rappelled down into the yawning blackness of the chimney, while Johnny Faulkner and I prepared the haul system.

My first implication that something was erring was when Kendal radioed from the abyss to start the raise, but do it very slowly. Monitoring the effect of the pull on the ropes, I noted there was an unusual tension. Suddenly, the strain disappeared and the haul line appeared to jerk free of something. Then a sharp message from Kendal to switch to a lower system. Johnny and I complied, although we had no idea of the reason. After a short wait, the raise command was given and in short order the body of a young man was hauled over the safety rails into the overlook. I did not learn the full story until Kendal and Butch ascended the chimney and rejoined us.

The young man had plunged head first into the crevice, wedging his head tightly in the narrow confines of a crack. Needless to say, death was apparently instantaneous. Kendal and Butch placed a rope around his ankles and issued the command to raise. The slack I had felt was the body jerking free from where it had been jammed. The lower was to bring the body back down in order to place in a stokes litter for the final journey to the top.

Another extraordinary incident at Chimney Rock was where a young man tried to jump across the crack and plunged into the chasm and actually lived to tell the story. When I received the call, a warning chord struck. Kendal had transferred to Georgia, Johnny had resigned from the team and Butch had taken a position in Louisiana, robbing me of my best team members. Arriving on the scene, I shouted down into the contumacious mass of the chimney and received no answer. I was not expecting one. Of the many falls here all had resulted in death. I rigged my gear and double checked my knots at that point stepped prudently over the edge into the half darkness of the stack. About 80 feet down I discovered a young man lying on a very narrow ledge and unconscious. A cursory examination revealed multiple severe injuries, but least he was alive. I was amazed and delighted. Due to the gravity of the injuries I decided on a litter lower plan. Always before I had raised the victims vertical (deceased) using a three to one haul system, but this time I needed to keep the victim horizontally due to the back injury. I radioed this information to the top, and I was soon joined in the crack by Dan Dourson and Al Cornett, with the necessary equipment.

We turned our attention to the patient securing him on a back board with a cervical collar. After this, he was placed in a stokes litter and tightly strapped to remain stable during the 100 foot lower.

Right away I noted a problem that caused some concern. I would need firm safe suitable anchors for securing the ropes. These were in short supply. I decided on a large leaning boulder Placing the anchor strap around the boulder, I tied down the strap in order to minimize slippage, attached a brake bar rack and passed two ropes secured to the stokes litter through the brake bar threading over and under the brake bars. This would provide friction enabling a lower to be carried out slow and easy. With this device I could also adjust the friction while in transient. Meanwhile, Al was rigging two safety lines on the litter as a backup while Dan stayed with the victim.

All was ready. I instructed Dan to attach himself to the litter ropes using a seat harness and a special litter tie-strap with a short piece of rope and a sliding prussik knot as a backup. I inspected the rigging and noted it all satisfactory. I explained to Dan (this was his first lower with a real victim) he would guide the litter and victim down the cliff face keeping it level and that I could adjust in either direction from the top at his bidding. Al would help get the litter over the edge and assist in the lower.

The slack was removed from the ropes, the litter moved over the cliff edge and the descent was initiated. Once over the edge, the operation became one of intense concentration on the brake bar rack and listening for Dan's instructions on correcting the level of the litter, and Al controlling the safety ropes. In this manner we lowered the victim and rescuer toward the valley floor.

After a few tense moments the litter touched down and Dan

called all was secure. Leaving Al to remove the lower gear, I immediately rappelled over the edge to check the victim. By this time other rescuers had crossed the river and made their way upslope to our location. One hour later, the victim was placed in an ambulance which raced to Clark County Hospital. All in all, the rescue had taken just under three hours, a very good time.

Miraculously, the victim recovered after a period of time and gained the dubious distinction of being the first person to fall from Chimney Rock and live to tell about it. It's an honor of sorts, but I don't recommend it.
It is ironic to find death and danger in the Red River Gorge, which for so many people is a celebration of life and creation.

How do these two incidents relate to the Sociology of SAR? Hopefully, with a brief look at some of the problems in Gorge SAR we may gain a better understanding of the social aspect of visitors to the area.

For all this to be meaningful, we must compile data from the accidents and separate into male, female and child. Abide with me over the next few pages, while I make an attempt to sort out the accidents by gender, incident and deaths. Also, a few of my own experiences as a long-term veteran of the Red River Gorge.

The Sociology of SAR is difficult to determine. From 1960-200, a 45 year span, 1653 SAR missions have occurred on the Stanton Ranger District. 80°% where male subjects 15% were female subjects, while 5% were children.

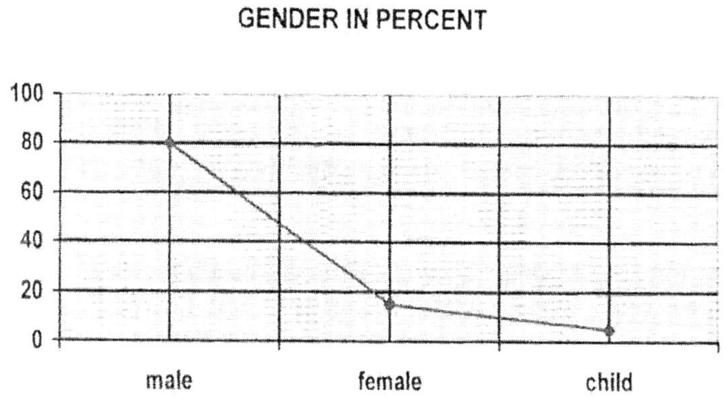

The above graphs the relationship between the genders. While this is not a true indicator, the male always appears to be more daring and apt to get himself into a hazardous situation. Most of the female accidents were in more of a controlled risk situation. Many of the child SAR's were lost, drowning, and unsafe acts permitted by the parents.

The sociology of SAR is therefore, a relationship between the visitor and how he behaves in the natural environment of high

cliffs and rugged terrain. It is also the relationship between the victim and SAR personnel

Just what is the social relationship between the victim and the SAR team? A victim is apt to be frightened and looks upon the rescue team as their salvation. This is hardly surprising since rescue, a form of divine salvation, is mentioned often in the Old Testament. In the parable of the 100 sheep, the shepherd leaves the 99 to search for the one that is lost. Since Jesus Christ equates himself as the good shepherd, with all the people as his sheep, this passage may be interpreted as the unselfish giving of ones self in order to help another in need, the motto of any SAR team.

What does the perspective of sociology offer to individuals interested in improving the effectiveness of SAR efforts? Not only should we be concerned with dealing with victims under stress, but an improved understanding of the social relationships among the rescuer and victim.

This may become clearer if we consider an analogy. Picture a topographic map. A very useful resource in our line of work. But what is a "topo map"? Maybe just a sheet of paper with wavy lines. Well, yes- - but the lines are not drawn in a casual manner. They are drawn precisely in relationship to one another so as to constitute a graphic abstraction of a given physical reality. Lines on the map can predict actual landforms. The abstract gives some indication of the actual landscape.

In an analogous sense, I am seeking to construct social maps-maps of social behavior of victims in a rescue situation, and to a lesser extent, their relationship with the rescuer.

For example, if we look at the following chart we may observe the number of SAR missions by type over the past 45 years

FALLS	1050	FROM CLIFFS
LOST	430	RESPONDED
WATER	68	WATER RESCUE
MSC	32	OTHER
FATALS	73	

Over a thousand incidents were falls from high cliffs where the victim was usually very traumatized and in fear for his life. Some 430 were lost or missing persons that may have suffered some form of trauma, usually fear of being alone, wild animals or injury. Water incidents were usually fear of imminent death, while miscellaneous varied from case to case. Death presents a highly traumatized situation.

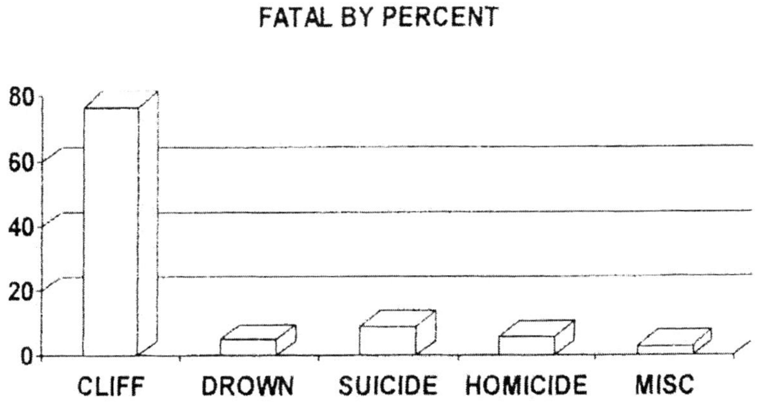

As depicted in the above chart 56 or 77% of the deaths recorded on the District were falls from high cliffs. Drowning were infrequent with 4 or 5%. One of these was a small child. Another was a young adult female and male. All occurred on Red River. While the chart indicates 5 murders, it appears that only one actually occurred on Govt property. (Chimney Top - near Princess Arch Trail) The other 4 it is believed, occurred elsewhere and were brought to the district for disposal, (i.e. Slade Overlook. Chimney Top Road. KY 715 near Gayhart cabin site) The district SAR team recovered the bodies which had been thrown over cliffs. These accounted for 6 % of the total. Suicides accounted for 7 or 9 %. They occurred on Chimney Top Road, Edwards Branch, Tunnel Ridge and Indian Creek. "They involved overdose of drugs, a self-hanging which involved a complicated suicide letter, vehicle exhaust fumes and self-inflicted 12 gauge shotgun wound. Miscellaneous indicates 2 or 2%. They involved Russian Roulette and a falling tree, both on Indian creek. Another shot himself twice in the chest and once in the head with a .38 revolver. Exposure was 1 or 1%. A young lady died of hypothermia before the rescue team could reach her on Parched Corn Creek. A total of 73 deaths have occurred in the Red River Gorge Area, including 3 by natural causes.

Examining the link between the SAR Team and the victim we will analyze the response of the rescue team of how many times have you seen these headlines in the newspaper.
"TWO DIE ATTEMPTING RESCUE OF DROWNING CHILD". If someone is lost, hundreds will search and often one or two searchers are injured or killed. But the next time someone is lost, just as many volunteers turn out to assist in any way they can.

Poor math...but very human. It runs through all our folklore, all human religions, all our literature--a racial conviction that when one human needs rescue, others should not count the price. Consider the following:

> In the name of God, the Beneficent,
> the Merciful...whoso saveth the life
> of one, it shall be as if he had saved
> the life of all mankind.
> The Koran, Surah V, 32

When I was a young climber in the early sixties, I recognized the element of society as a concern for the safety of visitors to the Red River Gorge. With this in mind, and ever increasing technological rescues, the Red River Gorge Mountain Rescue Team was formed in 1968 to meet the needs of huge visitor increases due to the Red River Dam controversy, a big issue at that time. So, rescue is a strong affirmation of the bonds of society. Usually, of course, it just takes the form of something that needs to be done.

Accidents are system failures. They should not be dismissed with some falsely heroic notion of "going for it" and losing. It is not good enough to say that "Jack would have wanted to go that way."--No one really wants to go. To meet our sociological goals, this must never happen.

Several years ago, a young lady fell from a frightful height at Eagles Peak. After a technical rescue lower, we started the long hike out with the stokes basket. (Did not have litter wheels in those days) I recognized the young lady had internal injuries, and

my thoughts were to get her to the hospital at full speed. To complicate matters, darkness had shrouded the land, along with a driving snowstorm that almost obliterated the trail. The young lady kept reaching for my hand in an effort to establish social contact. I refused the contact, intent instead, on getting her to safety. I did not realize, what she apparently knew, that her life was limited to a few precious moments. This social contact of joined hands was very important to her for this reason. I failed to recognize the significance of the contact, and continued forging ahead, eventually reaching the roadway and the waiting ambulance. She died enroute to the hospital of a ruptured spleen. When I was informed of this, I realized far too late what she was trying to do. Just contact and comfort with another human after a traumatic event. I wept openly, and vowed this would never happen again. And it has not, although I have never forgotten my preoccupation, on that long ago winter night, was so great that I refused to a dying lady the touch and contact of another human being which she so desperately needed.

I have learned, over the years, that the individual is small when compared with society as a whole. The social aspects of SAR are much more than a technical rescue or conducting a search. They involve the feelings and needs of the victim beyond the initial rescue. Not only to the victim but the rescuers as well.

SOCIAL CONTACT NEEDED

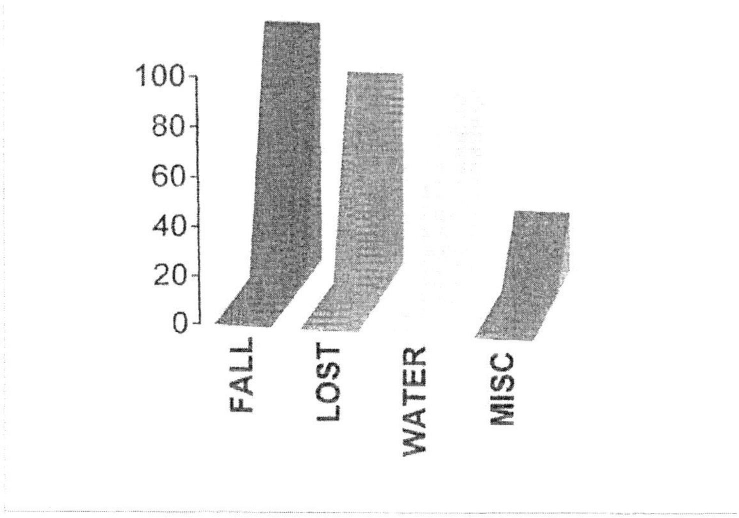

In reference to the above chart we can see that in the case of falls from high cliffs and being lost, most require 100% of social contact needs, while water related and miscellaneous per off somewhat. What does this tell us? A person suffering the trauma of a fall from a cliff or being lost has a need to talk about his experience. It many cases it seems a half-dream in which the person is outside his body observing the rescue, (as described by many of the victims). What is the SAR member's duty to the victim, aside from providing medical care and technological expertise? From discussion with victims, I surmised that the victim in many cases needs a personal contact with someone. A touch of a hand, or some physical reminder that things are under control and the ordeal will soon be over.

What of the social aspects of contact with an injured visitor? What of the needs of the victim for such contact?

The social contact summary is a first attempt to analyze the

need for contact on the victim's part after a high cliff fall or other trauma. This is especially true of serious injuries where the victim has a great fear of imminent death. Such victims deserve a special empathy and considerations.

SOCIAL CONTACT SUMMARY

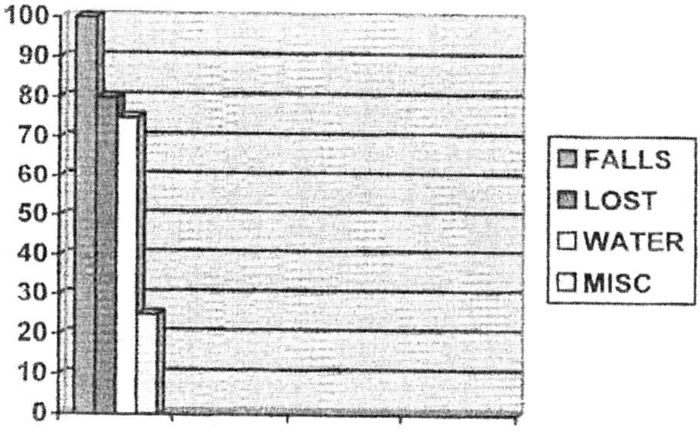

The chart is based on observations and conversations with a large number of accident victims in the Red River Gorge. While the methods used to obtain this information were very unorthodox, with no thought given to future value. It is nevertheless a beginning point to understanding victim behavior before, during, and after the accident. There is something about a fall from a high cliff, which emotionally affects different victims in dissimilar ways. It is far beyond the scope of this paper, and the author's ability, to expound on this subject.

The Sociology of SAR would not be complete without some analysis of accident prevention. Except for acts of nature, it is unsafe acts and unsafe conditions, or a combination of both that cause accidents.

UNSAFE ACTS AND CONDITIONS

Over 1650 rescue missions have occurred on the Stanton Ranger during the period 1960-2005, 1620 appeared to have been caused by unsafe acts, as compared to 30 which may be attributed to unsafe conditions. The unsafe conditions do not include inclement weather or acts of nature. Included are:

1. Bridge railings and decking
2. Uneven trail surfaces
3. Hazard Trees
4. Road surfaces
5. Overlook rails
6. Stairways
7. Fencing
8. Boulders

Aside from natural events, accidents are caused by unsafe acts or unsafe conditions. or more frequently a combination of both. To prevent accidents from occurring, unsafe• conditions must be removed, barricaded, or brought to the attention of the visitor. Since unsafe acts are the primary problem in the Red River Gorge. the visitor somehow must be persuaded not to commit unsafe acts.

We cannot remove the danger of high cliffs. We can only modify some of the conditions to make them less dangerous.

We can only hope to modify or partially control the behavior of the visitor to prevent unsafe acts.

A young man was in the process of a rappel, Australian style, near Rooster Point. The shock of the sudden taking up slack in the rope caused a carabiner to fail. The victim plunged 110 feet. The rescue was long and arduous I have kept a piece of the biner as a memento and a reminder of the frailties of human life.

The Rescue Team ultimately has a role when unsafe acts are committed. It is hoped a future document will be framed to chronicle the Team from training, where they learn the meaning of discipline, to actual rescues where they sample the price of unsafe acts.

The under 25 age group, to which most accidents have occurred, tends to be more adventurous, more imprudent, less experienced, less knowledgeable about outdoor hazards, and more likely to get themselves into an accident producing situation. They are lest likely to be restrained by warning signs and barriers than the older more prudent age groups.

However, only a relatively small proportion of the total number of visitors, act imprudently while in the hazardous environment of high cliffs. As might be expected most accidents occur during weekends and holiday period.

To help reduce and prevent accidents we should consider;
1. The need to give special attention to public safety and high cliffs.
2. As visitors continue to increase, it is imperative that public safety measures be intensified.
3. Making environmental systems safety analysis from the USER POINT OF VIEW of public use areas.
4. Consider SAFETY FIRST in all new plans.
5. Recognize that there are "risk seekers" and groups being formed called the "Right To Risk" and where they fit in.
6. Do we attempt to regulate or limit risk activities or do we value the benefits attributed, and so will encourage a measured amount of risk?
7. Examine the Kentucky Recreational Use Statute (KRS 411.190).
8. Incorporate the Risk Measure Matrix for all inspections.
9. Concerted effort to alleviate the problem of visitor unsafe acts in a systematic fashion.
10. Recognize that we probably cannot change human nature. We must accept human nature for what it is and plan accordingly.

11. Consider social behavior "maps".
12. Implement Preventive Search and Rescue measures (PSAR)
13. In reference to risk activities, help participants to appreciate the risk they are taking and prepare accordingly.
14. If risk activities are limited or not limited. how would this affect the ordinary visitor?
15. Educate visitors on negative aspects of risk.

LONG-TERM SEARCH OPERATION

"And the cares that infest the day
shall fold their tents like the Arabs.
and as silently steal away."
-Longfellow-

The sociology of SAR must include the affects of a long-term search operation on the searchers, relatives and the media.

Three prolonged search and rescue operations occurred in the Red River Gorge, within a three year period. One of the searches lasted 8 months, another about 3 weeks and an additional one lasted 3 months. This is in marked contrast to the typical search, which is generally terminated in a few hours or a night and day. Contemplate the affects on the family of not knowing the status of their kin for an extended period. They sometimes feel compelled to critique the search efforts. This can cause a destructive consequence on the searchers, who are volunteers anyway, and they may feel obliged (at least in their minds) to actually give up the search. Add media criticism to this and you have a social situation which is rapidly deteriorating.

A brief synopsis of each of the search incidents will foster understanding from the viewpoint of searchers, relatives and media.

January 1, 1981, a young male subject (19) wandered away from his camp barefooted in subzero temperatures with a blanket of snow on the ground. He was reported missing and under the influence of drugs by his companions. A 12 day search was hampered by harsh frigid weather. He was found on the 12th day, his body frozen solid at the base of a waterfall. It was necessary to chop him out of the ice very carefully. The death of this young man brought major criticism from the family for his icy demise, which created a focal point for the news media.

May 19, 1984. a young male subject (17) disappeared from his camp after a fight with another member of his party. His skeletal remains were discovered 8 months later by a grouse hunter. The discovery of the teen-agers remains came amid numerous rumors that the boy had been found previously--in Florida, in Winchester, and one comment was that he was found crucified in the Gorge. Family only mildly critical.

December 16, 1984. a male subject (24) came to the Gorge alone on Sunday, failed to report to work on Monday and was reported missing on Tuesday. His car was located in the parking area at the Wolfe/ Menifee County line. As in the other cases, airplanes, dogs, psychics, helicopters and other rescue teams were utilized. 3 months later two hikers reported what appeared to be a blue backpack at the bottom of a steep crack in the cliff. The rescue team located the remains of the missing subject a few hours later. Family very supportive of search and rescue efforts. Publicly expressed appreciation for the many hours of searching by the rescue teams.

Imagine the effects on a family as days, weeks and months pass with no sign of their loved one. This is bound to be a traumatic influence on their mental attitude. The old adage of "No news is good news" wears thin in this situation. The Indian Creek search occupied about 240 days, the Clifty search some 90 days, while Chimney Rock accounted for 12 days.

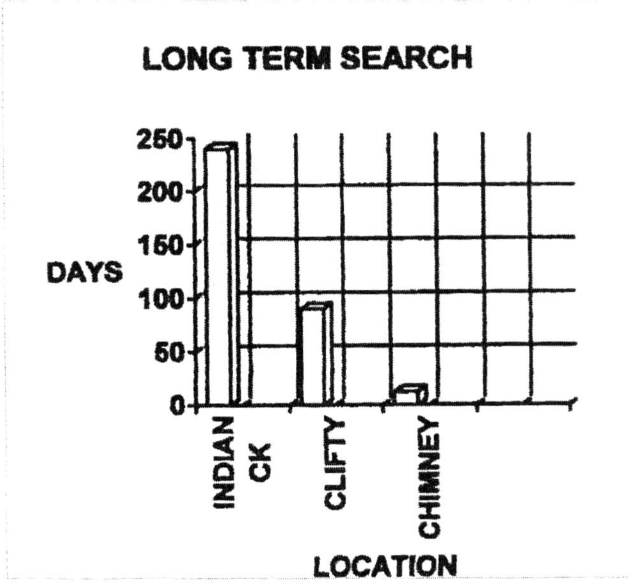

What is the sociological relationship between relatives and SAR, beyond what has been mentioned beforehand? The person in charge of the search should give a daily update to the family as a means of keeping them informed of progress. This was done on all the searches outlined above. Reaction of the families were mixed, with Clifty being one of gratitude and appreciation. Indian Creek was supportive along with a touch of cynicism. Chimney Rock was one of restrained animosity, as the family did not think enough was being done. However, some of the relatives did join in the search efforts as radio operators, record keeping and search map updates. These individuals performed a needed service as it released capable searchers from this duty and allowed them into the field. These individuals did not take kindly to the comments of other relatives. Since they were actively involved, they considered it a contribution to the search effort. Thus they felt a part of the incident and not just bystanders doing nothing. Perhaps active involvement is the key to abating some social problems before they develop.

What is the difference between these searches? All utilized typical search methods and procedures. The January search was conducted under very hazardous weather conditions (ice and snow) in a rugged terrain of high cliffs and precipitous drops, where the rescuer was in considerable danger.

The May search was conducted in warm weather, in rugged terrain with an abundance of poisonous snakes.

The December search was for the most part good weather. This was the largest search in terms of manpower. Use of dogs, helicopters and airplanes were similar to the others. Search area was in a hazardous high cliff area with numerous fissures, sinkholes, and deceptive cliff edges.

Censure of the search efforts by the family may be expected and justified when the search turns up nothing. It is not the amount of manpower in the field, the family sees, but rather the safe return of the victim. In their anger and frustration, they may vent feelings on the search teams. Such suppressed anger should be received in an empathetic way by the searchers.

In dealing with the media one must always keep a sense of proportion, balanced with the actual facts in contrast to hearsay. The media will ordinarily prefer the facts over what someone thinks or surmises.

A search is never officially terminated until the victim status is known. It is scaled down into what is called a Limited Continuous Search or LCS. Although active physical presence in the field is minimal, all new clues or leads are thoroughly investigated. A compromise of this sort accedes to emotional pleas by the parents to continue. The mission may be suspended but not the search. The case remains open.

An old adage may balance it out: "I did what I thought was right, no man could have done more." But is this really enough? Our society has changed immeasurably since those words were written. If you failed to find a victim before his demise, you may consider it a "well organized" search anyway. To the family, you have failed in the highest way possible. You have to keep a sense of proportion.

HIGH CLIFF ACCIDENT ANALYSIS

"Every man desires to live long"
Swift

An analysis of high cliff accidents indicated several different categories. Getting to close to edge of cliffs for various reasons accounted for 60% of the accidents. Legitimate climbers were low with 5%, while rappelling was 20%. Australian rappelling accounted for 3%. Slips were 2%. Miscellaneous showed 10%.

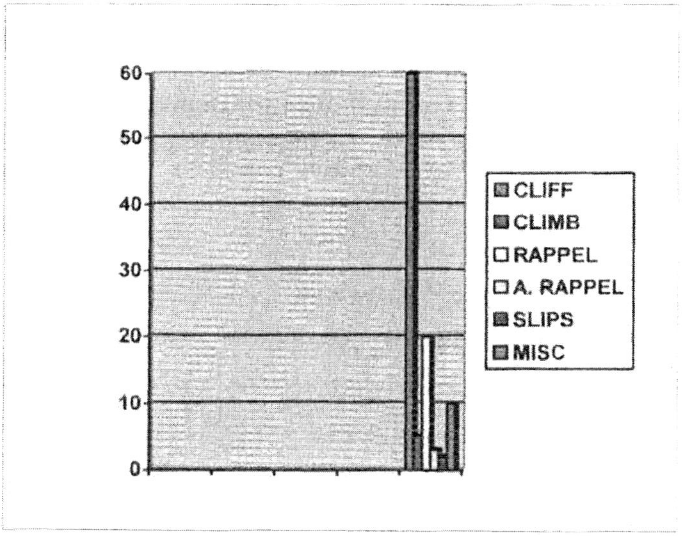

The miscellaneous category included such things as chasing a roll of toilet paper over a cliff, urinating over cliff, jumping across cracks, amateur rock climbing, falling into sinkholes, and various other unsafe acts.

The Australian rappel is one of the most dangerous forms of rope descending. The subject goes head first, without a belay, control of the descent is marginal at best.

Rappelling accidents included: Rappel without gloves (rope burns to losing control), getting long hair caught in rappel device, anchors came loose, harness failed. panic (letting go of rope), and the list goes on and on.

Legitimate climbers included; failed belay, protection devices did not hold, falling rocks, rock projectile broke.

Slips included things like leaf/moss carpet, rain slick cliff surfaces, winter ice, and various other things.

The cliff edge was responsible for 60% of the total accidents. The cliff itself is not an unsafe condition, being part of the natural environment. So unsafe acts were common such as:

1. Simply walk off the edge of a cliff during the night
2. Camping to close to the edge, rolling over cliff in sleeping bags, trying to stop burning logs from rolling over cliff, gathering firewood at night, placing wood on campfire close to edge of cliff, holding on to small tree or shrub and leaning over cliff, just to name a few.
3. One leans over cliff while another holds, causing them both to plunge over.
4. Sitting with legs dangling over cliff edge.
5. Sitting at the top of waterfalls.

These examples are just a few of the more unthinking things visitors do, without realizing there are certain dangers of which they must be aware. Such unsafe acts as wandering around at night without a light and setting up camp 2 feet from the edge of a 100-200 foot cliff indicates a lack of good judgment or just plain ignorance of the dangers that surround high cliffs.

The individuals who climb over the safety rails at Chimney Rock Overlook and attempt a jump across the 4 foot chimney crack is a study of visitor behavior at its most daring.

The social aspects of visitor behavior on the cliff edge is one in which daring individual's emerge who have never before been in

rugged country and do not know the precautions that should be taken. They strike out on their own, ill prepared for any emergency. And become victims, as it were, of their own ignorance.

This is not the case for everyone. Many outdoor people appreciate the risk they are taking and prepare according.

It falls to the lot of the Red River Gorge Mountain Rescue Team to search for the lost, pluck the injured from rocky cliff ledges and remove the dead.

Even a simple sprained ankle can be a major problem because of the rugged and hazardous terrain and the sometimes long distance to carry the victim in a stokes litter.

The most serious injuries were caused by high cliff falls. Types of injury varied, but the majority were spinal, head, broken limbs and internal. Emergency Medical Technician treatment covered other injuries where the patient was not transported to a hospital. First Aid treatment included minor cuts, bruises and contusions.

INJURIES BY CLASS

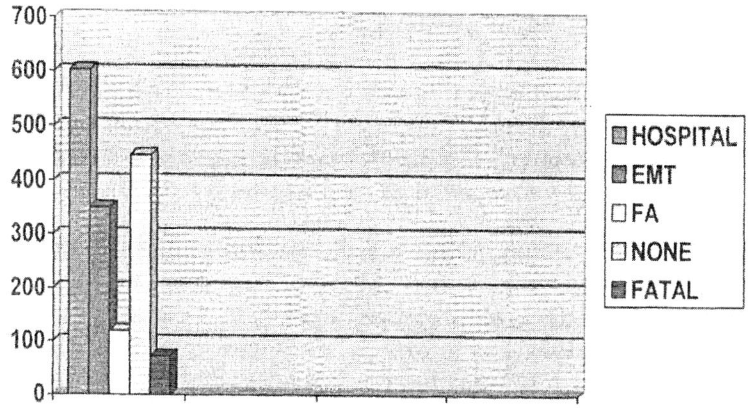

The "no injury" were mostly lost persons incidents. Follow up on the more serious incidents revealed that many of the victims were left with permanent disability of various body parts as a result of the fall. Some are paraplegic. Others are brain defective.

Initial treatment on the confines of a high cliff ledge is a far cry from ideal conditions, especially in inclement weather. In some instances the victim has to be secured to keep from going over the edge. The rescuer is always secured before any treatment or movement into a stokes litter starts. Working on a cliff ledge with 100-200 foot vertical drops is one of the most challenging and exacting of all rescue operations. The sociology aspect of SAR really comes into its own in these situations. The victim is injured, in fear for his life, and looking out over a deep chasm does little to calm his fear. Here is where the one on one situation (rescuer to victim) can be of primary' importance. The victim should be given an account of what is going to take place and the intended use of all the ropes he sees around him. Whether it be a technical raise or lower situation, the victim

will fare much better if he has some idea of what is about to happen.

A victim once remarked: "It's my life, see!" This is an interesting observation. Probably he had never read the Koran. To re-quote from an earlier chapter, Whoso saveth the life of one, it shall be as if he had saved the life of all mankind."

From the Old Testament comes a well-known and often quoted verse: "Am I my Brother's keeper"? This may soon become, "I am my Brother's keeper" if a trend towards imposing a general duty upon a bystander to assist a person in danger becomes a reality.

Since the early 1900's, it has been argued that an individual should have a legal duty to save another individual from bodily harm if he can do so without inconvenience to himself. This arose in reaction to the countless situations in our country where victims of accidents or sudden medical problems were left unattended by bystanders. Despite the continued occurrence of such incidents, our legal system has not yet prescribed any general legal duty to aid a person in danger. We have only a moral duty to help another in need. However, the trend towards imposing a general duty upon the bystander to assist a person has been gaining momentum.

Most states have already enacted hit-and-run statues imposing a duty on a driver involved in an accident to stop and render assistance to any person injured in an accident.

Similar statues impose a general duty requiring individuals to report incident of child abuse, and the Good Samaritan statutes protects the individual from liability providing he does not exceed the extent of his medical training. (i.e. person trained in basic first aid, should not try to treat a patient in the same manner as an Emergency Medical Technician).

The concept of the "Good Samaritan" was developed from the biblical parable told by Jesus. According to the parable, a Jewish man was robbed and beaten by thieves, than left half-dead by the side of the road. Several people passed by, including a priest, and saw the man but refused to help him. Along came a man from Samaria, and stopped to help the injured man.

The concept of the "Good Samaritan" is alive today and is one of

the prime factors motivating SAR.

But what of the Sociology of SAR? What does it offer? Hopefully an improved understanding of the social relationships between the rescuer and victim. The safety of any adventure is directly related to the knowledge of and preparation for its hazards.
As SAR members, we must continually improve our own skills and actively seek to promote a better understanding of a hazardous environment and social relationships.

Only in this way can all of us achieve our goal of safe, effective rescue. Or go even a step further and put the SAR Team out of business due to a lack of demand for its services. This should be the goal for all teams.

Some social relationships develop over a long period of time and are constantly changing. Social realities reflect patterns, which are sometimes relatively short-lived. An organization may be formed shortly before an election for the primary purpose of getting a certain individual into office. After the election, it disbands, regardless of its success.
Similarly, a SAR Team, formed for a special service, would disband when that service was no longer required. While it lasts, "the patterns of social behavior" has important implications for the victims and team members involved.

No SAR mission is ever exactly the same as any previous one. Nevertheless, different high cliff SAR missions present somewhat similar types of problems. Thus, by constructing social maps we can provide a future SAR Team with specific behavior patterns of victims in a rescue situation.

The old adage, "you can't see the forest for the trees", becomes a reality when an SAR Team focus most of their planning efforts on a single tree-their own organization.
We must modify our thinking to include the entire forest. In this way we will see and understand the social behavior patterns of not only the victim, but the team as well.
Until the day comes when the Red River Gorge Rescue Team is no longer needed, we will be in there, doing what is required, with special empathy and consideration for the victim.

Am I my brother's Keeper?
-Genesis IV:9
How think ye? If a man has a hundred sheep, and one of them be gone astray, doth he not leave the ninety and nine, and go-eth into the mountains, and seek-eth which is gone astray?
-Matthew X11: 12-

How much then is a man better than a sheep?
- Matthew XVIIt12-

Each year we gain a little. You have to keep a sense of proportion. The use of Preventative Search and Rescue, PASR, for short, has been a successful effort over the years to prevent and minimize as many dangerous situations as possible, through public education, training and use of signs. This is a very fundamental social aspect of SAR. PSAR is actually a crucial core element and really should be implemented before the other four: locate, reach, treat and evacuate. An event or rescue where the scope and complexity was limited by the immediate actions of the victims, is the best of SAR missions.

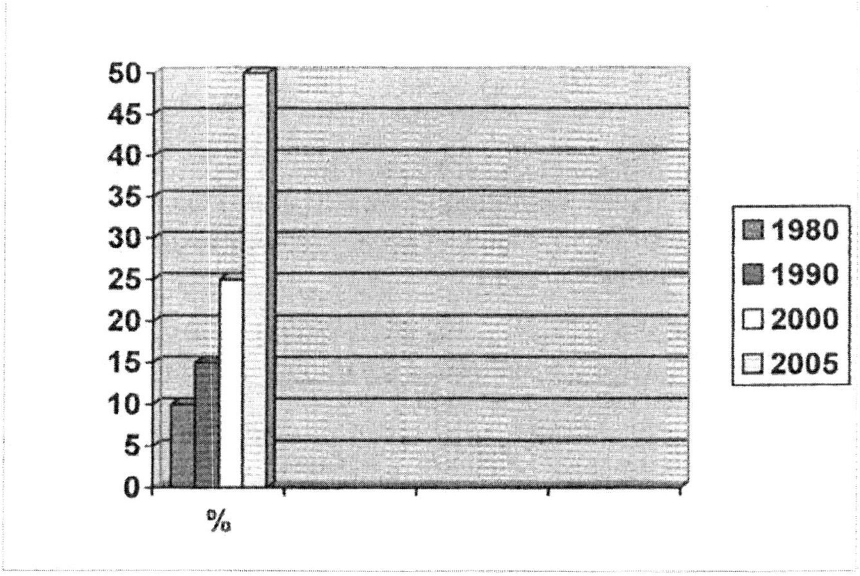

The use of PSAR was first tried in 1980 where about a 10% reduction in accidents occurred. 25 years later this climbed to a 50% reduction in average per year SAR missions.

FENCE THE RED RIVER GORGE?

"One ear heard it, and out the other out it went."
-Chaucer-

The following refrain was sent to me anonymous in the early seventies when a movement was about to fence the gorge due to the large number of falls from cliffs. It is interesting from a sociological point of view in that it brings out fictitious fractions in a dead lock about a controversial point. Needless to say it would border on the ridiculous to attempt to fence hundreds of miles of cliffs. However, the author (whomever it might be) takes the approach of a parable in fencing the gorge or having an ambulance down in the valley in a humorist kind of way. If we look beyond the quipster rhyme, we can see the social implications of this poem in that two components are at work here: Accident prevention and rescue. The author, in some far seeing moment, described the situation decorously as opposing views of those who would fence and those who would not.

The old sage came close to the truth when he lamented that too much attention is given to repairing results than to stopping the cause. This philosophy was met with scorn and the sage was ridiculed for his viewpoint. Called a fanatic, his outlook was contorted to the point of including charities. However, the author concludes, "To rescue the fallen is good, but 'tis best to prevent other people from falling."

The following chart graphs an informal survey on to fence or not in the early 1970's: (Fencing the Red River Gorge was actually an issue during this period)

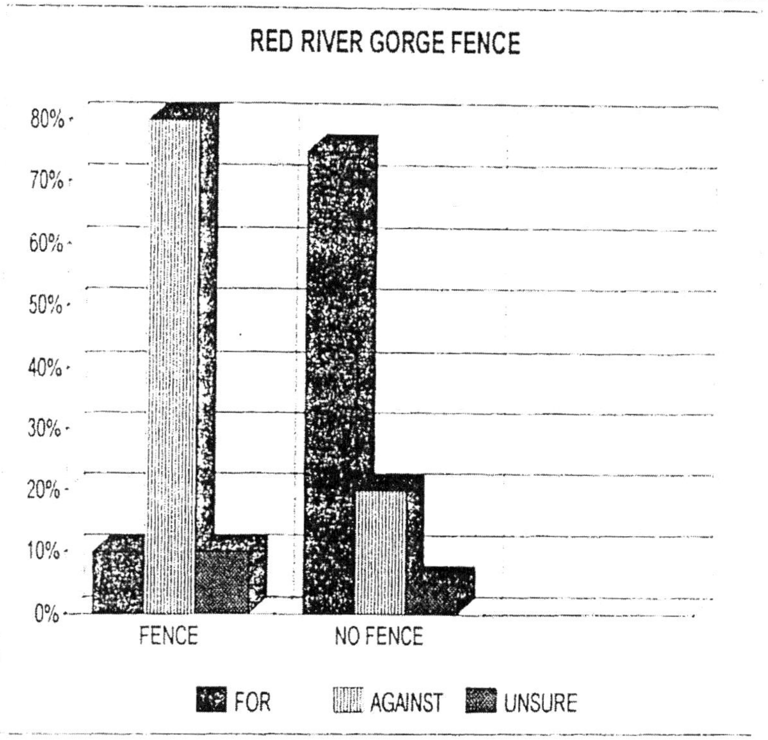

RED RIVER GORGE FENCE
80%
70%
60%
50%
40%
30%
20%
10%
0%
FENCE
NO FENCE
FOR
AGAINST
UNSURE

A FENCE OR AN AMBULANCE

"Twas a Dangerous Cliff, as they freely confessed,
Though to walk near its crest was so pleasant;
But over its terrible edge there had slipped
A duke and full many a peasant.
So the people said something would have to be done,
But their projects did not at all tally;
Some said, "Put a fence around the edge of the cliff,"
Some, "An ambulance down in the valley."

But the cry for the ambulance carried the day,
For it spread through the neighboring city;
A fence may be useful or not, it is true,
But each heart became brimful of pity
For those who slipped over that dangerous cliff;
And the dwellers in highway and alley
Gave pounds or gave pence, not to put up a fence,
But an ambulance down in the valley.

"For the cliff is all right, if you're careful," they said, "
and, if folks even slip and are dropping,
It isn't the slipping that hurts them so much,
As the shock down below when they're stopping."
So day after day, as these mishaps occurred,
Quick forth would these rescuers sally
To pick up their victims who fell of the cliff,
With their ambulance down in the valley.

Then an old sage remarked: "It's a marvel to me
That people give far more attention
To repairing results than to stopping the cause,
When they'd much better aim at prevention.
Let us stop at the source all this mischief," cried he, "
Come neighbors and friends, let us rally;
If the cliff we will fence we might almost dispense
With the ambulance down in the valley."

Oh, he's a fanatic," the others rejoined,
"Dispense with the ambulance? Never!
He'd dispense with charties, too, if he could;
No! No! We'll support them forever.
Aren't we picking up folks just as fast as they fall?
And shall this man dictate to us? Shall he?
Why should people of sense stop to put up a fence,
While the ambulance works in the valley?"

But a sensible few, who are practical too,
Will not bear with such nonsense much longer; T
hey believe that prevention is better than cure,
And their party will soon be the stronger.
Encourage them with your purse, voice and pen
And while other philanthropists daily,
They will scorn all pretense and put up a stout fence
On the cliff that hangs over the valley.

Better guide well the young than reclaim them when
For the voice of true wisdom is calling,
"To rescue the fallen is good, but `tis best
To prevent other people from falling."
Better close up the source of temptation and crime
Than deliver from dungeon or policy
Better put up a strong fence round the top of the cliff.
Than an ambulance down in the valley.
-Anon-

SAR INCIDENTS BY SEASON

" Know then thyself; Presume not God to scan
The proper study of mankind is man"
-Pope-

From a sociological viewpoint the incidents by season may have important significance to chronicle the activities that draw people outdoors and the hazards they are likely to encounter. The following chart is graphed into falls from cliffs, lost, water, miscellaneous and fatalities. It is further divided into seasons of the year.

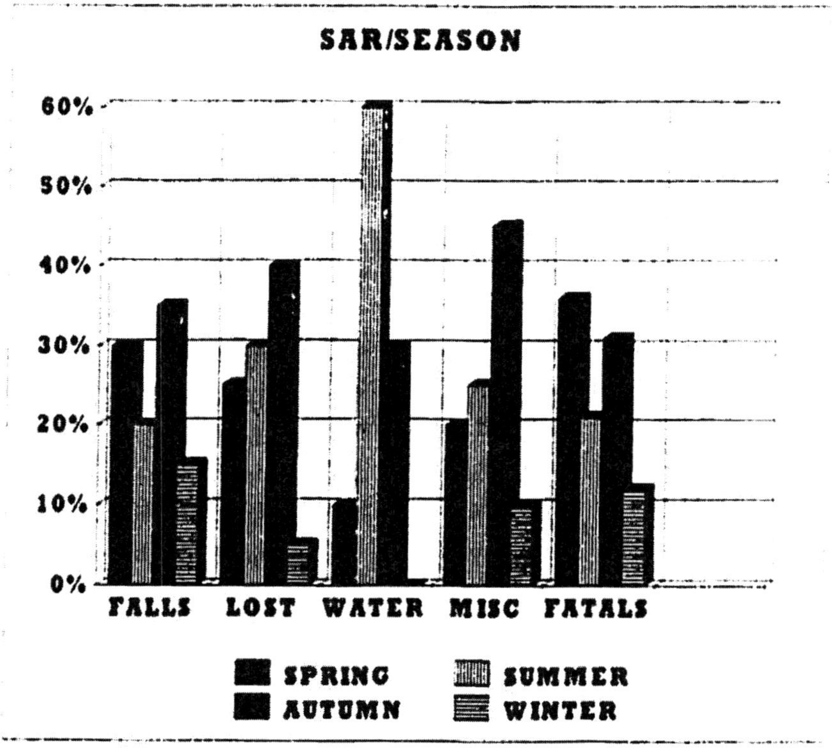

What does the than indicate about the social relationships of people as far as outdoor activities are concerned' The season of the year has a

direct bearing on the outdoor use of an area. The accident rate increases proportionately to the number of people, and the seasons determine the visitation.

There appears to be two social problems facing the visitor and rescue communities. The first is that rescue has become very technological and has created a special class of rescuers, linked with the fact the average visitor knows very little about how to get themselves out of trouble in the forest. The second problem is that rescue has become a specialized service provided free by a government agency or an industrial society. The federal government is required, either by law or recognizing its public duty, to assist anyone asking for help. The type of response depends upon the individual situation, but there will be a response of some sort. The cost of these rescues is paid by tax dollars, and so far has not been passed along to the rescuee.

The situation is in need of a change. Unthinking or uncaring individuals are causing unnecessary risks to lives and property as well as costing all taxpayers money. Ultimately, the people will be responsible for new restrictions that will unjustly affect all Red River Gorge users.

The logical solution is to move the moral burden of responsibility and financial accountability back to the user. The end result must be that each of us be held responsible for our own actions while in the forest, just as we are held responsible for our actions while driving on the highway. The federal government should not have to bear the burden of negligence.

The USFS undertakes search and rescue missions not as a mandate but rather as a public duty to render assistance. There is no statute imposing a duty, the breach of which would be actionable at law.

We have tried in the Gorge to insulate visitors against a host of environmental and societal dangers. Numerous regulations have been established with the primary focus of public protection. Ironically, as we strive to counteract hazards and jeopardy, thousands of people seek out risk and danger through their recreation.

In other words risk or the threat of physical harm emerges when there is a loss of control over the outcome of a particular activity. Although some may picture the seeking of risk as dangerous and foolhardy, many recreators view risk-taking as a desirable and even necessary basic for their enjoyment.

The objective is not to completely eliminate the risk but rather to manipulate it to acceptable levels. This is accomplished by including personal skills and abilities, correct decision-making and proper equipment. A certain amount of risk is reputed to have great therapeutic and educational values. The participant uses element of danger to accomplish certain feelings and objectives.

This brings out an entire new concept of social relationships, that of the risk-takers and where they fit into the sociology of SAR. What of the "right to risk" groups who say they do not want a rescue mounted if they are injured? The sociological implication of such groups is far beyond the scope of this report. However, history does tell us that man has learned to apply himself virtually and achieve dominance over his environment.

The Bible begins its account of human history outside Eden with man condemned to "Till the ground and earn his bread by the sweat of his brow." Whatever their beliefs, values and social structure, all men must meet the demands of the environment if society is to survive. Man must act on the environment, either adjusting to it or dying in it.

The "Right to Risk" groups forming in different locations contend the value of a wilderness experience is the right to risk life and limb. Basically, they want self-sufficiency and claim they will self-rescue without any external help. Very little else is known about this movement except they are in their early twenties. I would think they would reconsider a helping hand should they be seriously injured and facing the "chilling hand of death." Time will tell. It will be interesting to see how the "rights" of this group will affect other visitors to the Gorge. Where does one group or individual rights stop and another group or individual rights begin?

Some sociologists contend the breakdown of established social and cultural forms and the emergence of new ones is a process that is continually going on. Different groups in society are affected differently by social change. Some groups are disposed to oppose change and others to promote it.

How does all this relate to the sociology of SAR in the forest environment? This is an absorbing question and I ardently await the explanation if there may be one.

SAR MISSIONS BY SEASONS

"Nothing in this life became him like the leaving it;
He died as one who had been studied in his death;
To throw away the dearest thing he owned,
As it were a mere trifle."
-Shakespeare

It may be interesting to examine the sociological relations between accidents and the season of the year. Spring is often a time of exhilarating renewal and feelings of a new start in life. Summer usually brings feelings of well-being. Autumn ushers in the death of a season and for many people it is a period of melancholy and at times despondency. Winter often yields periods of depression and suicidal thoughts especially during holiday periods. Certainty, we all have our moments, the spring, summer, autumn and winter of our lives. If we examine the following graph, we find that most accidents occur in the spring and autumn. This is hardly startling since a large portion of the victims are under 25 years of age and this is the spring break period for colleges prompting a large inflow of young visitors to the gorge. Autumn brings slippery fallen leaves and the largest flow of visitors to the Red River Gorge. This is to be expected since nature often puts on a colorful display of color with the leaf change.

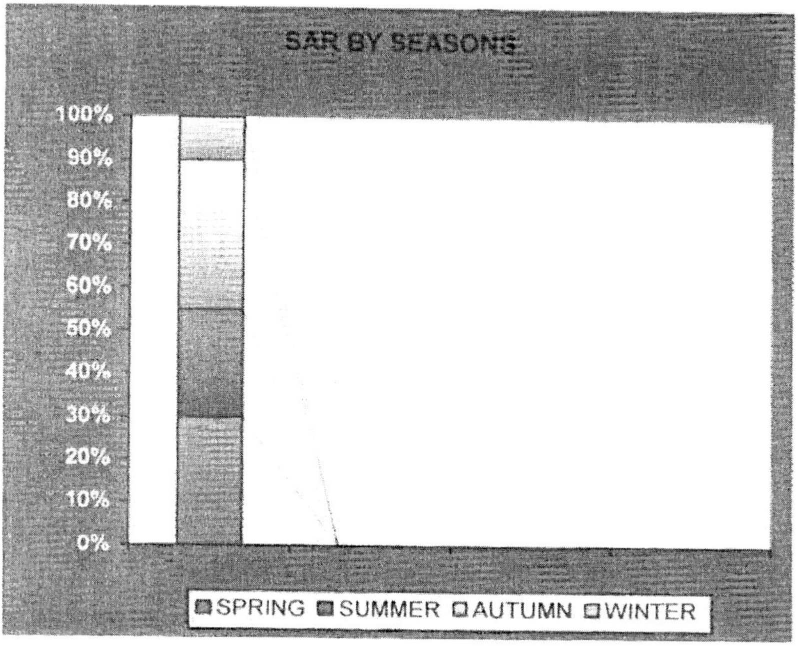
SAR BY SEASONS
100%
90%
80%
70%
60%
50%
40%
30%
20%
10%
0%
SPRING
SUMMER
AUTUMN
WINTER

Fatalities show a similar story except for the 12% occurring during the winter months.

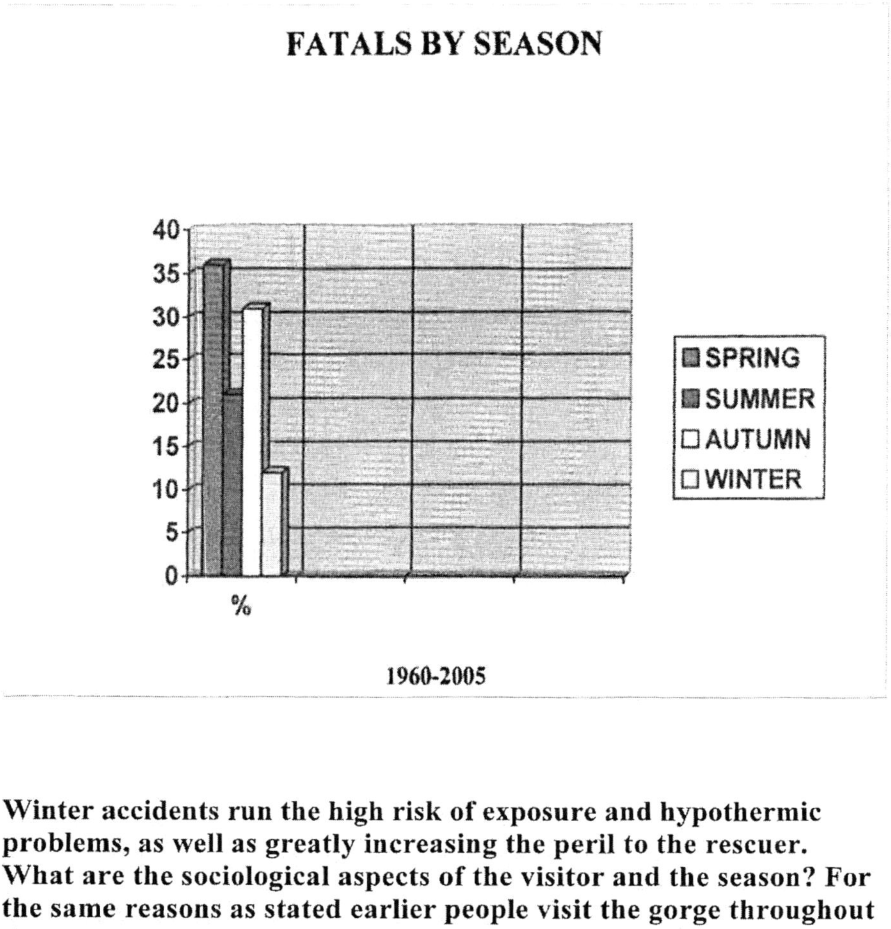

Winter accidents run the high risk of exposure and hypothermic problems, as well as greatly increasing the peril to the rescuer. What are the sociological aspects of the visitor and the season? For the same reasons as stated earlier people visit the gorge throughout the seasons and each term has its own special attractions. Many people adapt well to the changing seasons, while others are affected in various ways such as depression and discouragement

The social impacts of the seasons is a get away from the ordinary day to day routine to gather with friends or family in an outdoor setting

of exquisite beauty no matter what the changing season. Since it has been determined through statistics the under 25 age group are more likely to be involved in accidents, add to this college students on spring break feeling their freedom and independence, along with high cliffs of the gorge and you have a ready made accident scenario. 34% of the accidents and 36% of the fatalities occurred in the spring primarily in this age group. 32% of the accidents and 31% of the fatalities occurred in the autumn. As might be expected the accident rate increases proportionally to the use. Summer yielded 27% of the accidents and 21% of the fatalities, while winter tallied 7% and 12% respectively. While some may consider this an aberrant comparison, it is listed purely for the sake of education and preparedness.

HOME OF VICTIMS

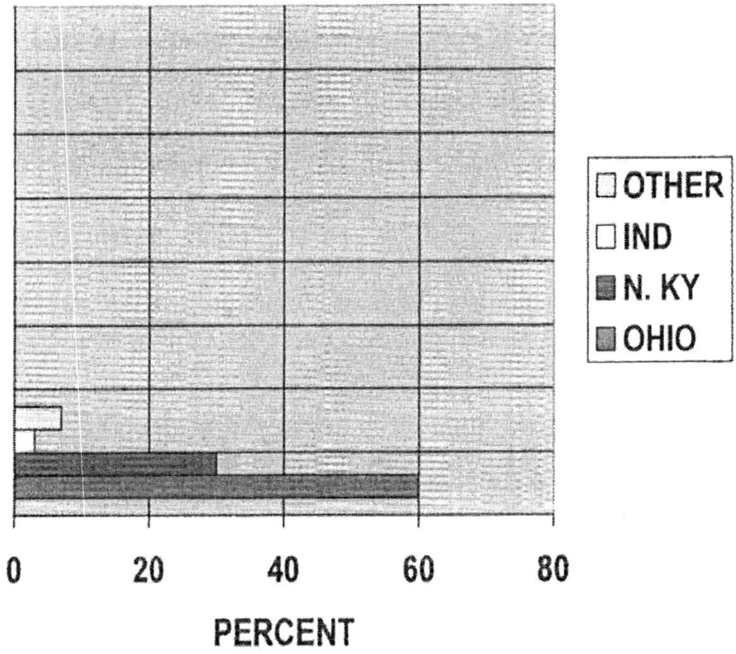

The chart above graphs the demographics of the victims: 60% of the visitors were from Ohio, 30% from northern Kentucky, 3% from Indiana and 7% from other states and one foreign country as listed below:

MI	**ALA**	**NY**
RI	**CA**	**ILL**
VA	**TX**	
ENGLAND		
WVA	**PA**	
FLA	**WI**	

Throughout the changing seasons only the cliffs remain the same. Even this is not completely so. Differential weathering is constantly at work deepening and eroding the land in minute quantities, grain by grain. In our short and hectic lifespan, the changes are not apparent. But in the age of geological reckoning, they are happening at a rapid pace. For an untold number of years the forces of wind, water and temperature have been in the process of sculpting the mysterious beauty of the Red River Gorge. It is ironic indeed that death and danger exist alongside the grandeur.

The very thing that brings the visitor here such as sweeping vistas, high cliffs and unparalleled scenery also bring exposure to hazards in spite of warning signs to the obvious dangers. When people learn to heed the warning signs, stay on the trails, and never never try to jump across the crack at Chimney Rock, plus not climb over safety fences, than we are truly near our sociological goals of disbanding the rescue team.

When that day comes, there will be no need of "A fence round the top of the cliff, or an ambulance down in the valley." as the anonymous author of the rhyme, A Fence or an Ambulance relates.

I am reminded of another story: On an exquisite autumn night when it seemed you could almost touch the stars, a young male subject was admiring the night sky when he stepped over a cliff backwards near Sky Bridge. Johnny Faulkner and I responded, along with Gary Hawkins. Looking over the cliff and calling, we heard a faint response. Finally, we could make out a ledge about 50 feet below the rim. Johnny rigged his gear and stepped off the edge into the enveloping blackness of the chasm. He reached the ledge without incident and reported the young man alive with no life-threatening injuries. Good news indeed, this rescue was going well. Hawkins and I prepared the raise system and passed on to Johnny what equipment he requested. The 3 to I raise system was somewhat difficult to place owing to the angle of the pull. I solved this problem by adding directional pulleys. All was ready, awaiting a signal from Johnny. The raise commenced slowly and carefully. About three-fourths of the way up the cliff, Johnny calmly commented that one of his Gibbs Ascenders had come loose. Alarmed, I stopped the raise and locked it off. I was preparing to rappel down to Johnny when I heard him say to the victim: "Hold this light, buddy." Whereupon Johnny secured himself, reached down and attached the ascender as calmly as if he had been on terra firma. He grinned up at me and announced, "I'm ready, let's go." I breathed a sigh of great relief, unlocked the system and continued the raise. A few brief moments and the victim, along with a still grinning Johnny, came over the rim.

I have seen many of his amazing feats over the years. It was almost like a ballet on ropes. He was astounding in his skills and is sorely missed.

RELIGION AND SAR

"Help yourself, and Heaven will help you"
La Fontaine

Way, way back in the 10th century, a young man decided the day before his wedding to give up worldly pleasures, join the church, and spend the rest of his life helping those in need. This young man was Bernard of Menthon. He struck out for the Alps where he founded a monastery by a pass and trained large dogs to assist him in rescue efforts. By virtue of all this service he became known as St. Bernard and the progeny of his dogs bear the same name today. This ideology of self-sacrifice and assistance to others fostered the development of the search and rescue team.

The rescue community has close bonds to society as a whole. Some of the most ancient and elemental tales are stories of search and rescue. This may come as a surprise, but rescue (usually a form of divine salvation) is a major theme of the Bible. The Old Testament tells of the angels rescuing Lot from Sodom just before its destruction. Hager and Ishmael were rescued by angelic revelation after being cast out by Abraham. The New Testament relates the travels of Luke and his care giving to those in need.

In Matthew, Jesus Christ relates the parable of the shepherd who leaves his 99 sheep to go and search for the one that is lost. Since Christ equates Himself with the good shepherd, with all the people as His sheep, the passage is interpreted as the unselfish giving of oneself in order to help another in need. That there should be a strong tie between religion and search and rescue should come as no astonishment, since salvation is one of the fundamental principles of most religious traditions.

Search and Rescue missions, no matter how carefully planned or executed, are subject to failure. As these missions are often characterized by emotional involvement, this disappointment can sometimes bring scrutinizing human injury. However, the part played by religion in the functioning of human societies should not be underestimated. It is still true, as Burns aptly put it about the "best laid plans of mice and men."

All this indicates the concept of search and rescue has been an integral part of society since recorded history. Of course there have been many changes in technology and equipment. On a modern day rescue, with helicopters overhead, radios crackling, and ropes strung everywhere, I sometimes wonder if old St. Bernard is looking down on us and wondering what he and a bunch of mongrels started so long ago.

Whatever the case, the ultimate goal of all SAR teams is to be put out of business due to a lack of demand for their service.

Rescue, like religion, acts out a heroic epic of defrauding death. There are Old Testament accounts of sages and tribes lost in the desert. Rescue stories of Helen from Troy and the Quest of the Holy Grail.

One account of this quest is given in the poem "The Vision of Sir Launfal by James R. Lowell. A young maiden knight is preparing to begin his search for the Holy Grail. On the eve of his departure, as he sleeps on a bed of rushes, he has a vision or dream in which he sees himself as a knight in shining armor riding forth on his quest. He sees himself tossing alms to a beggar at his gate, but at the same time shrinking from the old man. The Grail, he assumes in his dream, is to be found at the end of wonderful adventures in distant lands.

Later he again sees himself in a vision. This time he is a gray-haired old man returning after a life spent in a vain search for the Grail, only to find his castle occupied by another. Once again he finds a beggar at his gate. This time, the old knight's heart now being filled with love and humility, he recognizes in the beggar a poor fellow mortal and shares with him his crust of bread and a drink of water from a wooden bowl. A light shines all about the place and the beggar stands before him glorified. The bread and water have become a sacrament and the wooden bowl has become the Holy Grail. Sir Launfal awakes from the dream to realize that "The Grail in my castle here is found." In astonishment, he declares, "Hang my idle armor up on the wall, let it be the spider's banquet hall. He must be fenced with a stronger mail, who would seek and find the Holy Grail."

The experience of the vision changes the young knight's nature. Straightway he puts into practice the spirit of brotherhood of man by sharing the wealth of his earldom with the humblest of his fellowman.

The quest for the Holy Grail, the cup from which Christ drank at the Last Supper, was a vision shared by many of the Knights of the Round Table. Although the corporeal Grail was never discovered, there were many deeds and rescues associated with this religious journey.

In the historical experience of man and the development of human societies, faith and rescue have shared a common bond in empirical beliefs upon which religion rests.
We all have our quests, either real or mythical.

THE ELEMENT OF RISK

"If this belief from heaven be sent, if such be Natures holy plan,
have I not reason to lament, what man has made of man?"
-Wordsworth

Once in a blue moon a team comes together that really clicks, whether it be in music, sports or search and rescue. Such a team molded in the Red River Gorge in 1978 and faded into obscurity a few years later. But while it lasted, it was truly a team of magnanimous dimensions where everything just came together and functioned as the team never has before or since. It marks the first time since its origin in 1968 that the rescue team was comprised of all Forest Service volunteers. Being all members of the same organization formed a social bond of unusual significance. Briefly, let us look at the part played by SAR in the functioning of human societies and of its contribution to individual personalities.

As we noted earlier, there is a strong tie between SAR and religion. There is also a strong bond between members of a team when they are working together for the benefit of society. Rescue team members recognize that death, pain and suffering characterize the very existence of their profession. They are face to face with situations that carry them beyond the established and defined situations of ordinary social behavior. For example, on a high cliff rescue where you are guiding a stokes up a precipitous cliff supported by only a few thin ropes, and the victim of a head trauma starts to become combative. Even if the litter straps are tight enough to restrain the patient, the attempt to thrash about (victim is usually not aware) in the stokes can upset the delicate balance of the already precarious situation, causing the litter to rock. This is a very dangerous circumstance as the seesawing can cause the ropes running across the lip to move back and forth across a sharp edge in spite of rope protection devices. As any climber can attest, a taut rope and cliff edges is a disaster waiting to happen. The members guiding the litter up the face of the cliff recognize the danger but are powerless to do anything except try to calm the victim. With a head injury this can be difficult. However, the rescuer is aware of the risk before he begins the ascent of the cliff, knowing full well that many things can go wrong. It is accepted as a controlled risk where everything is made safe that can be made safe.

Why do individuals take such controlled risks? In most cases it is a genuine desire to help those who cannot help themselves, and because society and religion is geared to helping our fellow man. It has been thus down through the ages.

What is risk? The definition will include words like chance and probability, but let's look at two types of risk: Perceived and Objective. A perceived risk is in your mind, an objective risk is where conditions are right for a risk. Any endeavor contains both. For example, if you rappel down a cliff UNKNOWINGLY into a den of rattlesnakes, the perceived risks are low -you don't know the snakes are there. The objective risk is high because of their physical presence and chance of snakebite. If you rappel down the same cliff in the MISTAKEN belief you have landed in a den of rattlesnakes, the opposite it true.

Risk should not be confused with peril and hazard. Peril is the source of the loss, a fire, a broken rappel rig and a liability in judgment are examples of sources from which losses may occur. They give rise to risk but are not risks themsel[v]es. A hazard is a condition that increases the probability of loss. Physical hazards would include a well worn rope, the summit during a storm and a defective climbing harness. Human hazards would include being accident prone, carelessness and a failure in judgment.

That some people should deliberately choose to engage in life-threatening recreation activities should come as no surprise to anyone involved in SAR. A large element of our society has as need for excitement, which comes from a degree of personal risk. Whether this might be your first rappelling experience or making the decision to climb Tower Rock, this may help you become a better citizen and a more satisfied individual because of this learned ability to develop confidence and overcome fear. Individuals can grow through experience and coping with risks.

These things usually fall into three categories: Psychological, social and physical. History shows that some people crave excitement and a degree of personal risk in order to fulfill certain psychological needs. Visitors to the Red River Gorge are participating more often in risk activities. People apparently wish to test themselves and the Gorge offers a spectacular background for spectacular feats of human achievement.

There are certain negative aspects of these activities:
1. Potential conflicts with other users.
2. Legal liability.
3. Environmental damage.
4. Potential of injury or death.

Many outdoor people appreciate the risk they are taking and prepare accordingly. While at the same time the Gorge is used by people who are unaware of the potential outdoor hazards, who strike out on their own ill prepared for any emergency. Who become, as Johnny Faulkner always said, victims of their own ignorance? These are the people who fall from cliffs, get lost while hiking, victims of careless accidents and the list goes on an on. As stated earlier, this is normally the "under 25" age category and more often then not, college students on spring break. Social patterns emerge because people appear to have a need for them. While some of this age group seek alcohol and drugs, others with a more positive stake in society embrace the quest for community and a search for new meaning.

Risk taking is nothing new. Individuals have always pursued this type of activity. It offers the participant excitement without competition and personal achievement while often in a unique natural setting.

Risk has been shown to have educational and therapeutic values. The participator uses elements of danger to accomplish certain objectives and feelings. Things like thrills, adrenaline surges, and what Maslow described as the peak experience of a self-actualizing person.

The Forest Service attempts to make visitors aware of the potential outdoor hazards by:

1. Signs
2. Newspaper articles
3. Regulations.
4. Television Programs.
5. Internet.
6. Interpretive programs.
7. Preventive Search and Rescue (PSAR).

While some of the Red River Gorge accidents are plain and simple accidents, a growing number appear to be the result of faultily equipment or the improper use of such accouterments. When we examine outdoor activities we sometimes find the device used or the improper use of such equipage can be almost sinful.

And the Bible cautions us about the wages of sin.

Yet the same type of accident happens over and over, as if no one has learned from past mistakes. Or perhaps it is the feeling that it just can't happen too me! The files contain many such cases. Whatever the reason for repeated accidents, when situations like this continue to occur, many times public pressure demands action from the responsible agency. Action means more rules and regulations. It should be that society holds the individual responsible for his own actions rather than forcing governing bodies to accept the responsibility.

Search and Rescue is an admirable thing, when one considers incurring considerable risk in order to help someone. Add to this there is a very real possibility of death or injury to the rescuer. It is a fine pursuit to help a fellow human and the poets write of the noble aspect of doing good. Yet, in reality, there is a distinct gap between philosophy and the chilling apparition of death on the high cliffs.

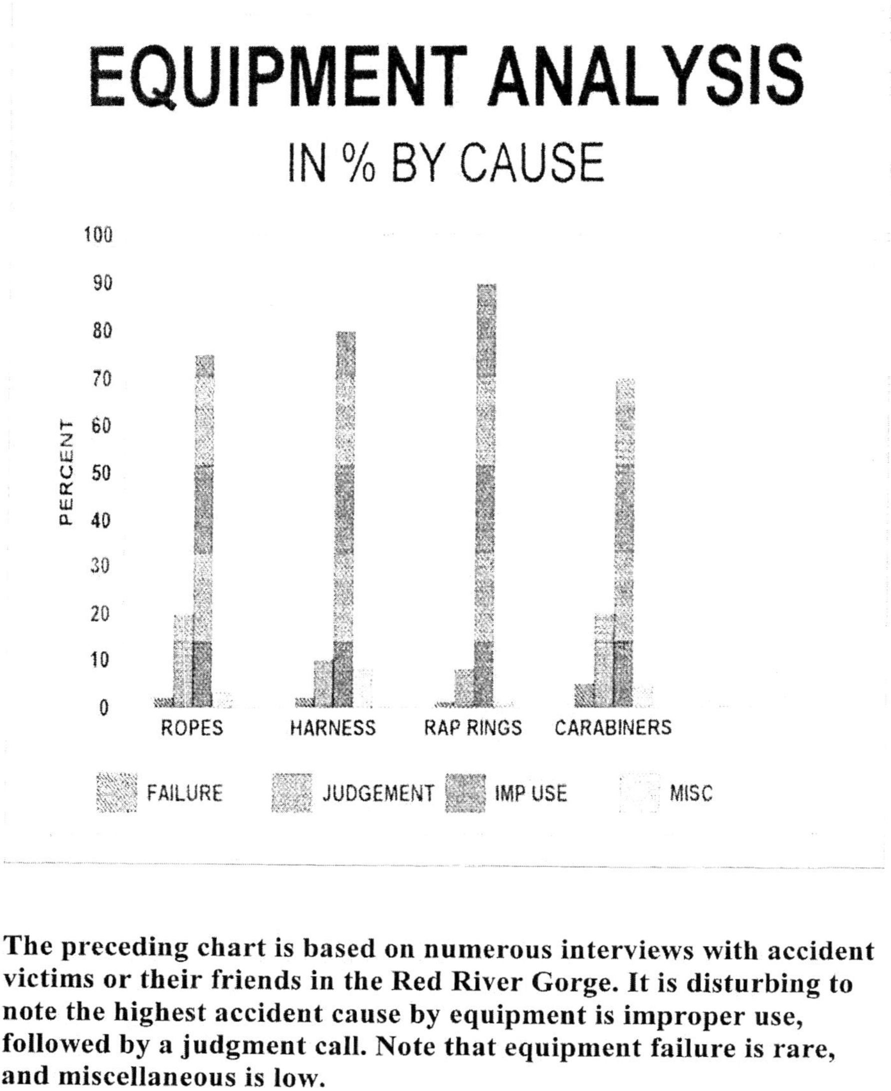

The preceding chart is based on numerous interviews with accident victims or their friends in the Red River Gorge. It is disturbing to note the highest accident cause by equipment is improper use, followed by a judgment call. Note that equipment failure is rare, and miscellaneous is low.

Most of the equipment on today's market is safe if used in accordance with manufactory's instructions. However, you must bear part of the burden yourself, such as regular inspections. Always use protection there the rope runs over the cliff edge Whether you are on the big walls of Eagles Peak, or the chairlift at Natural Bridge State Park. The rope makes the job possible. No matter if it's rappelling, climbing or moving a stretcher, your access route is the rope.

It is obvious the rope, as well as all other equipment, protects the rescuer and victim alike. You are literally "hanging by a thread".

High Cliff rescue, rappelling, climbing and the training involved are hazardous, risk taking activities. Each situation has its o n unique conditions and must bee valuated by those at the scene. Effective risk management comes from experience, proper training and good judgment. It is the user's responsibility to obtain competent instruction, choose quality equipment and use adequate safety precaution.

It is tragic that visitors can not or will not get proper instruction in the use of equipment. It is also of paramount importance to inspect all gear because it is subject to age, use, abrasion. and some chemicals. Retire old or worn equipment immediately.

How do you instill social virtue in the young? People have no moral instinct. They are not born with a moral sense, but acquire it through training, experience and sweat of the mind. A moral sense is an abstract of the instinct to survive. There are those who contend that the basis for all morality is duty, a concept with the same relation to group that self-interest has to individual.

in 1908 .1.13. Ames urged that a legal duty he adopted to reflect and reinforce the moral obligation to help one's neighbor. He apparently assumes that society benefits when it adopts legal rules that bring our system of law into harmony with our moral principles. While moral principles play a significant role in our legal system and have tremendous influence on the creation and development of legal rules, not all moral obligations should be declared as legal duties. It is generally agreed that the

"Common notion of morality" is an intuitive concept, meant to be a measure of the moral reaction one person is likely to have to another person's behavior.

Two states, Minnesota and Vermont, have passed legislation, which creates a general duty to perform "easy rescues", or "riskless rescues." A riskless rescue is defined as a dangerous condition that

another can alleviate without risk or harm to ones self or others. Another proposal is designed to reward and praise. This alternative would promote and encourage rescue without infringing upon principles of individual liberty and privacy which are threatened by legislation that enforces a moral duty to act with legal sanctions.

Others observe that society's interest in enforcing moral obligations may conflict with other values that a free society must respect. Lord Devlin suggested that before a proposed legal duty to enforce a moral obligation is enacted, society must balance these conflicting interests. On one side of the balance is society's interest in enforcement which includes deterring and punishing "immoral" behavior.
On the other side of the balance is a series of limiting principles.

A free society may not ignore its limiting principles without disserving the interests they are designed to protect. Society benefits when the Law interferes only minimally with the individual citizen.

Assume you are <u>not</u> a member of a rescue team. A small child has fallen over the cliff and is clinging to a sapling. You could reach her, but not without undue risk of substantial personal harm. If you ignored the risk and rescued the child, the common notion of morality would approve and praise the successful rescue. Moral sanction would not follow from the failure to act, except from your own ethics.

A small child has wandered near the edge of a high cliff. No one but you notices the child at play. You could easily remove the child from the danger zone without risk to yourself. The common notion of morality would approve the successful rescue and sanction the failure to act. If you had failed to respond, and the child fell over the cliff and was killed, the moral outrage created by the "Bad Samaritan's" indifference, would demand society deter similar future behavior by punishment. The "Bad Samaritan" is defined as a person who fails to offer assistance to someone in distress.

On the other side of the balance would a duty to rescue unduly interfere with society's interests in personal privacy or individual liberty?

All this is somewhat diverging from the sociological theory of SAR, but it may help the reader understand the difference between the rescue team member and the ordinary citizen concept of "the common notion of morality."

The common law does not recognize a duty to aid someone in distress even though the danger may be great and the inconvenience to the potential rescuer only slight. This presents an interesting, rather perverse situation. A potential rescuer who attempts to render aid must be cautious. If he in any way is negligent or intensifies a victim's injuries, a court may find him liable to the victim. The potential rescuer who does not lift a finger to help has no such worries. The law will absolve him of his callousness. He may be styled as a ruthless savage and a moral aberrant, but he is not liable for damages.

Way back in 1859, John Stuart Mill in his essay, On Liberty, advocated a philosophy which focused on individual liberty and the idea that individual freedom, that is unrestrained by government intervention, is essential for the progress and well-being of society. Mill's theory, commonly referred to as "excessive individualism" has been noted by critics to be seriously lacking in its refusal to recognize there are minimum moral requirements that must be maintained for a society to function. This is directly dependent upon adherence of the law to a binding moral code.

Excessive individualism is where the individual reigns supreme and the community is secondary. Proponents of Mill's view argue that courts do not have the authority to direct people as to their conscience. Critics claim that society must and frequently does impose considerable limitations on the right and activities of its members, a necessity for its very survival. As times change and morals change so should the law.

It would appear the duty of a bystander to rescue someone in distress is not a legal one, but falls into the realm of the instincts of humanity that require him to do so.

On Tunnel Ridge a young lady fell about 80 feet from a high

cliff and landed on a ledge 40 feet above ground level. When I reached the mantle by rappelling down from above, I found the victim conscious but very pale and bleeding from the mouth. Suspecting internal injury my first thoughts were stabilization and quick removal from the ledge. By this time a considerable crowd had gathered on the cliff rim, and I heard a most comforting voice, "I'm a doctor and I can rappel. Do you need any help?" I was in dire need of help as visions of a former rescue involving another young lady, whom I had failed, clouded my mind. I called up to the Good Samaritan doctor, that I would be most grateful for any assistance he could render, and at the same time asking one of the team members to provide the doctor with gear and belay from the top. Shortly the good doctor arrived and under his direction and assistance I was able to stabilize the victim for her journey upward in the stokes litter. The lady did have serious internal injuries, but thanks to a caring doctor she survived the ordeal and made full recovery. She owes her life to this medical wizard who prefers to remain anonymous.

MAN'S DUTY TO MAN

"Wake Duncan with the knocking! I would thou couldst!" -
-Shakespeare-

What is man's duty to man? Under the earliest Jewish Law, a man was held exactly accountable for any injury he caused another. If he knocked out a man's tooth, he must suffer the loss of his own tooth; if he took a man's life, he must forfeit his own life. It was the obligation of the injured man or his family to administer the punishment. Yet in the Sermon on the Mount, Jesus of Nazareth warns "1 a have heard that it hath been said, "An eye for an eye, and a tooth for a tooth:" But I say unto you, that you resist not evil; but whosoever shall smite thee upon the right cheek, turn to him the other also."

The transcendent rescue team finally came to an end. Transfers and attrition took their toll, leaving many "empty saddles in the old corral." as the old song laments. I can still look out on this mythical corral and see names emblazon the imaginary saddles, and remember the social structure that worked so well in SAR for the Red Riser Gorge. Replacement of this team was a difficult job and was almost an altruism, changing the sociological arrangement of the team. In time it balanced out, yet the team has never functioned quite well since. There was, for a term, a significant loss of solidarity; old groups in which so individuals find security and response tend to break down and new groups must form.

After the passing of this team it was necessary to modify the structure and accept new members while maintaining old traditions. One of the first tasks facing the new crew was a report that someone had fallen over a cliff near Sky Bridge. The problem was no one knew for sure where he was. After much chasing about, we located the area of the accident many miles from where we started. Talking to the subjects friends, they said he gone to look for firewood and had not been seen for several hours.

Part of the rescue team went down a nearby cliff to see if he had fallen over. Their surmise was correct. He had fallen about 90 feet and collided-head first-into a large rock. Apparently he had been walking down a small stream when he slipped on the moss under the water. He slid along the inclined creek bed until the water -and he- came to the cliff edge and over both went. Removing the body was a substantial

task which tested the team and formed the first social bonds of the new contingent.

Not just the victims suffer from these accidents: those who love them must attend their funerals and adjust to life without their physical presence or push their wheel chairs. Many people are disabled for life by their accidents.

The enigmatic aspects of the Sociology of SAR can sometimes be monumental in light of all the different missions and their affect on so many distinct people.

EMOTIONAL IDENTIFICATION

"Once more into the breach, dear friends, once more!"
-Shakespeare-

What are the social aspects of empathy of the rescuer for the victim? Emotional contagion occurs in a wide range of phenomena, including the drama of high cliff rescue missions. This is referenced by sociologist as a common mood, a state of mind affected by emotion. This appears to heighten suggestibility whereas people tend to look to others for clues, which in turn can he intensified by the presence of emotional tension, informal observations, based on man, years of perspicacious field notes, contrived the following analysis:

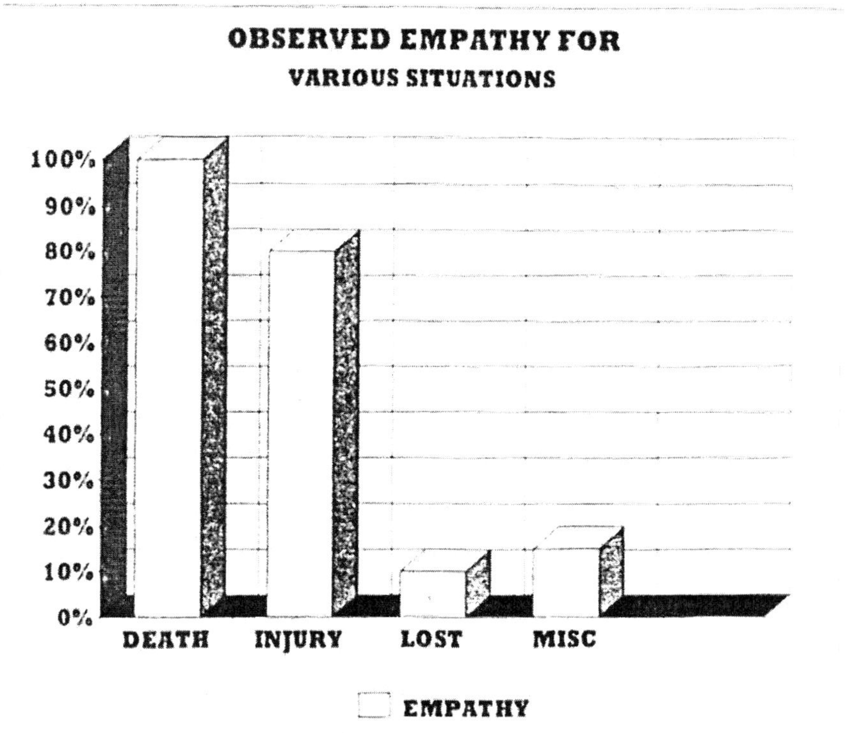

Note that death is 100%, followed by injury at 80% while lost and miscellaneous trail at 10% and 15% respectively.

This observation has no scientific basis. It is simply the result of field notes over almost 40 years of observing the emotional state of team members during rescue situations. As members have changed due to attrition, the chart reflects an average of the attitudes of many team members over the years. The results are hardly surprising since death in any form is a highly traumatized situation capable of producing a startling range of emotions. Little difference was detected between deaths causes (high cliff, suicide, etc). The head or spine injury created the most concern as these injuries often have lasting effects. Lost and miscellaneous were usually regarded as routine.

SOCIAL RESPONSIBILITY

"If a task is once begun
Never leave it till it's done
Be the labor great or small,
Do it well or not at all."
-Anon-

Moral virtue or social responsibility cannot be instilled in person who doesn't have it, doesn't want it, and resents having the burden thrust on him. Social responsibility above the level of family requires imagination --devotion, loyalty, and all the higher virtues--which a person must develop himself. If it is forced on him, he will retch it out.

As has been emphasized so many times before, the rescue team member is a volunteer, there because he chooses to be. The rescue team requires loyalty and a great devotion to the Red River Gorge. There is no better place to team and fine tune social responsibility than teamwork on the precipitous cliffs, working toward a common goal of reaching and evacuating the victim. The teamwork required on these rescues is phenomenal. Each member must trust another implicitly. With trust, comes loyalty and all the other higher virtues.

A good example occurred at the Sky Bridge area during the darkest hour of night. A young man had fallen over a 100 foot cliff and was grievously injured. Kendall and another team member, who is best left anonymous, rappelled down into the stygian blackness of the chasm. After insuring they were safety down, I began to rig the raise system. Kendal started treatment of the victim and preparing him for transport to the top.

The cliff edge was causing me some concern. It had an overhanging lip just right to hang up a stretcher. Well, I would deal with that problem if and when it was time. The raise started well but quickly deteriorated into a near hazardous situation. The lines used for climbing back up with the stretcher became entangled into the haul lines, due to the rotation of the stretcher on the way up. As we neared the top, I could now foresee a problem with the twisted lines sliding smoothly over the lip.
To add to the confusion, one of the team member's prussik knots or Gibbs Ascenders became jammed and he was stranded on the rope. His panic stricken voice called for help. Meanwhile I had

successfully maneuvered the stretcher to the lip, where Kendal was able, in spite of the twisted ropes, to crawl over the victim, and reach the top, where he quickly rigged another line to rappel back down to assist the other team member, who was only momentary stranded and in no immediate danger. Kendal made another successful rescue, but the team member thought his time had come and did not want to chance it again.

Remember, a volunteer can quit on a momentary notice and all that happens is you are short a team member.

I vividly recall a rescue at Chimney Rock resulting in the death of a young man whom had fallen while trying to jump across the crack. His leap to the chimney section was successful, but when he tried to return, his jump failed by a narrow margin and he plunged into the constricted confines of the chasm. After removing the body from a ledge, we started down the slope carrying the Stokes Litter (No wheels in those days), to Chimney Top Creek. Evacuation plans called for Chester Morrison (a resident of Chimney Top) to meet us at the creek with a tractor and farm wagon to transport the victim to the old swinging bridge. After we crossed the creek, the victim was placed in the wagon and the journey to the bridge began. As the tractor began to roll, the rescue team hitched a ride. On the way out we turned to a magnificent view of Chimney Rock, golden in the setting sun. I shall never forget the faces of the emotion laden young men as all eyes turned toward this spiny prominence, each deep within their own private thoughts.

I have seen this same look and utter stillness many times, since that long ago autumn day, after a fatality. It is a norm for the rescue team to chatter among themsel'es after the mission is completed about how well or bungled the sortie. After a fatality, this abnormal silence prevails along with a somber mood. I have observed it time and again in death situations.

The final rites of placing the victim into a body bag is long remembered experience, and one not looked forward to repeating. The ancient Chinese Taoism brought forth the belief that an individual could transcend nature and even life and death. A fine thought but one with no supporting facts. "It isn't the fact that you're dead that counts, but only how did you die." comments Edmund Cooke. There is really no middle ground. You are just as dead from an auto accident as a high cliff fall.

The reaction to a serious injury is one not only of empathy, but also of medical curiosity as each team member is seeking to add to his repertoire of knowledge in treating injuries under oftentimes adverse weather and precipitous cliff walls. Much discussion follows such injuries concerning treatment on the spot and a prognosis of recovery. This is in marked contrast to a demise where there is no recovery.

I shall never forget that long ago winter rescue of a young lady who had fallen from Eagles Peak and died enroute to the hospital of a ruptured spleen. She wanted only social contact of holding someone's hand. But I refused her offer, intent instead on getting her to the ambulance and not recognizing her grievous injuries.

I was young at the time and in the infancy of my career. Hopefully, I have learned something over the years and will never again be insensitive to a victims needs.

SAR MISSIONS BY DAY OF WEEK

"So stick to the fight when you're hardest hit,
It's when things seem worst that you mustn't quit"
-Anon-

When do the rescues happen? Some 80% of them occur in the dark of night. If you refer to the following chart the indications are: Saturday 60%, Friday 20%, Sunday 15% and weekdays 5%. The significance of Fridays is that visitors are arriving, sometimes late. In many cases they do not have adequate lights and blunder over deceiving cliffs. By Saturday they have usually established a campsite, often on the very edge of a high cliff. Getting up during the night to answer natures call and stumbling over the cliff is common. Sundays are usually holdovers from the night before, weekdays and nights are generally uneventful. Why do they happen? They happen to the untrained, the inexperienced, to those who think accidents cannot happen to them, and the ones who consider accidents as a matter of fate or luck. Carelessness and overconfidence are usually more hazardous than deliberate accepted risks. Most accidents are caused by mistakes, which could have been avoided. Risk and danger will always be present in the Gorge, but a good point to remember is to take no unnecessary risk, and make everything safe that can be made safe.

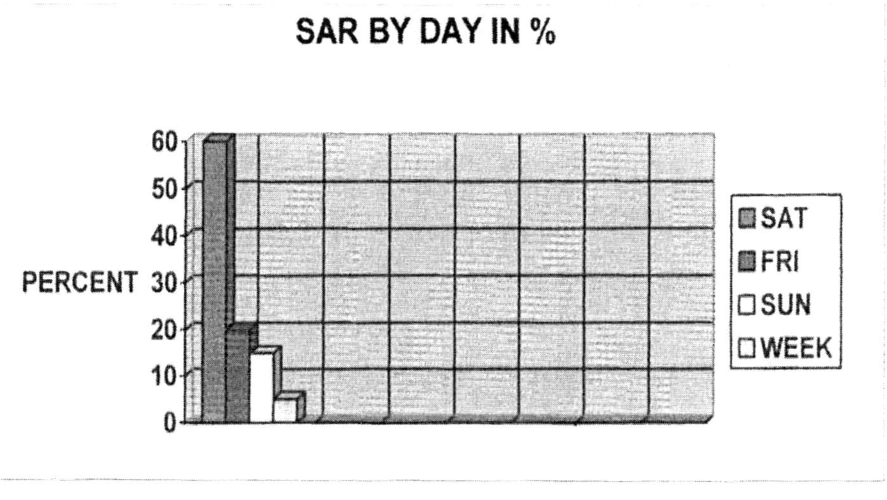

THE CONTROLLED RISK

"Early and provident fear is the mother of safety"
-Burke--

To make the assumption that rescuers plunge into a situation with a reckless disregard for personal safety in order to save a victim in distress is highly erroneous. There are many risks in any SAR operation, but especially in the high cliff realm. Risk is an inherent part of SAR, but they are never taken lightly. Everything that can be made safe is made safe before the operation begins. This is called a controlled risk. An evaluation is made of possible risks, and measurable action taken to control or diminish them. It is highly important that every team member be skilled and ready to take over any another team member's job if necessity dictates, the circle of completeness of Yang and Yin.

Of course every risk cannot be taken into account and must be dealt with as the situation ordains. The controlled risk is a safety factor and must never be ignored or maligned. Immediately upon arriving at a rescue scene, while the gear is being assembled, an evaluation is made of the risk factors that can be confirmed at the time. Steps are taken to minimize or abate these risks prior to commencing the rescue operation. These may be as simple as placing rope protection devices, or a directional pulley in the haul fines. Or it may involve complicated measures such a high lines or unusual rigging. Whatever it takes, safety of the victim and rescuer is the uppermost concern.

The team member is in an unenviable situation. There are certain jobs, in which he has specialized, but yet he must be ready on a moments notice to take over the task or another member of the group a group is sometimes defined as "any collection of persons who are bound together by a distinctive set of social relations. In the SAR community the social bonds are tight because of this unique order of morale "everyone works, everyone fights" The team members do not buck for a soft job. There aren't any!

Some types of rescue situations are more intrinsically dangerous to the rescuer than others. if we examine the following chart, we find that High Cliff rescue imposes a danger rating of 100%, followed by water rating of 70%. This chart applies only to the Red River Gorge where water rescue is minimal Lost persons

apply a rating of 30% while chairlift is 50%. Miscellaneous ranks 20%. This chart was formulated after interviews with many Red River Gorge rescuers over a time period of some 30 years. The percent of danger represents the consensus the rescuer gave to each activity as being the most dangerous. 100% represents the most hazardous situation and was unanimously given to high cliff rescue.

RISK TO RESCUER BY
TYPES OF INCIDENTS

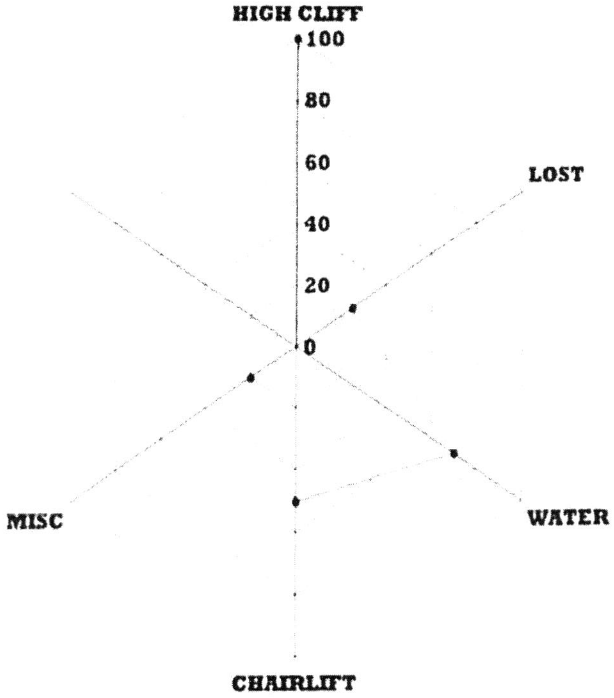

THE ONES WHO WAIT

"They also serve who only stand and wait"

What is a rescuer's duty to his home and family? Certainly, the ones who wait are oftentimes besieged by concerns for the safety of their husband or son engaged in a SAR mission. To leave loved ones in the caliginous night for an encounter with a high risk rescue on a sheer cliff wall is the undiminished embodiment of the National Search and Rescue Motto: "So that others might live!"

This is all noble and befitting the rescuer, but what of his long suffering spouse who may have endured this for years. The following chart is based on informal discussions with kin of rescuers and their reaction to different missions as a degree of concern:

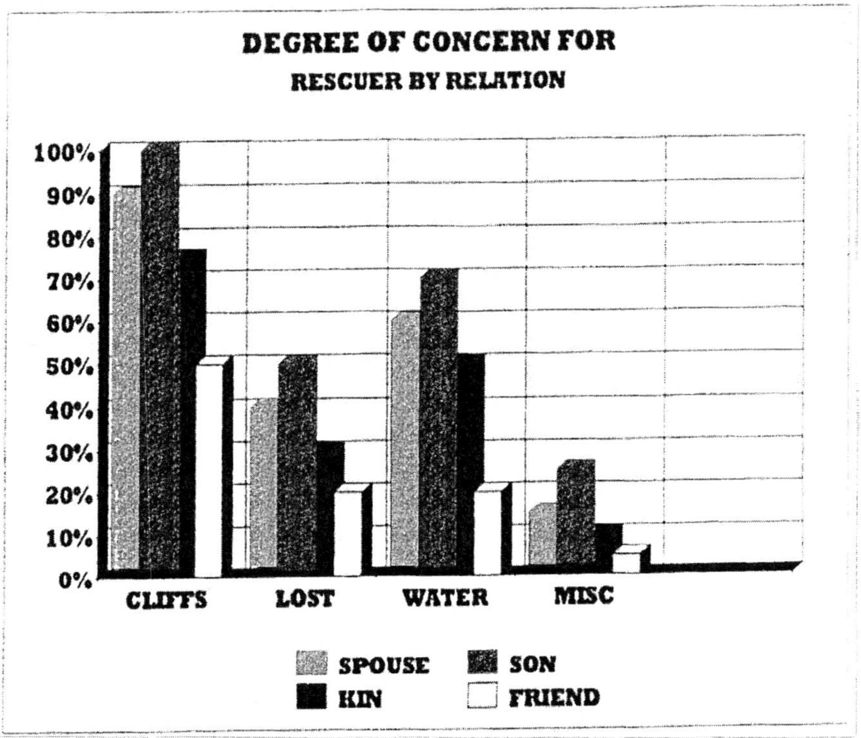

As indicated by the chart, high cliffs rescue cause the greatest amount of concern for the rescuer's family, Kin and friends. Individually, the concern for a son is highest among the ones who wait for the completion of the mission. Water rescue ranks second, lost third and miscellaneous fourth. The husband ranks second in concern while Kin and friends are third and fourth. This is, of course, dependent upon many factors, such as knowledge of the rescue operation, degree of risk to the rescuer and experience.

Social organization is comprised of interpersonal and group relations. The family is a unit of social organization in which a father is usually dominant. Thus the father is considered generally to be able to take care of himself, which would appear to account for concern rank of the son. A wife or female is regarded as naturally nonassertive and passive, the husband or male as naturally aggressive and active. The more passive and yielding a woman, the more feminine, and the more dominant a man, the more masculine. This theory has suffered a slow erosion over the years.

How does all this relate to the previous chart? Simply this. Looking at a high cliff rescue through feminine eyes, one may see the husband as in control and highly confident of success. While another may see her son through passive eyes and think he is not grown up enough to accept the controlled risk one must take on a high cliff rescue. Thus her degree of concern is oftentimes greater because the son, in many cases, has not had the experience. The son may also still be the "baby boy" to the mother.

While all this will not alleviate the concern, nor should it, the family will have for the member engaged in high cliff rescue. To pluck a victim form a precipitous cliff wall is the most exacting of all rescue operations. The team member is a volunteer, there because he wants to be. You can't coerce him -- you can't even keep him if he wants to leave. He can quit 30 seconds before a mission and all that happens is you are short one member. The volunteer is a free person. All that drives him comes from inside --that self-respect and need for the respect of his peers and his pride in being part of the team called morale, or esprit de corps.

Nothing, of course, will lessen the apprehension of the family until the safe return home of the rescuer. Many families are concerned with the risk factors, even though they are controlled risks, to the extent possible. Others worry about the unseen probabilities that are present on every rescue. Still others ponder the feasibility of SAR for people whom are seemingly inappreciative of the effort.

My loving, suffering wife, Susie, has endured over 1500 SAR missions with nary a word of complaint. In fact, she operated the only radio system available in the early days, long before the advent of a central,24 hour dispatch center, and was the team's only link with other agencies. To individuals such as Susie, is owed a special debt of gratitude. They are the real backbone of the team.

The family is a basic unit of social structure, a pattern of behavior associated with a distinctive social position, i.e., that of a father. Social organization produces social control mainly because people are dependent on each other. Thus the family of an SAR member may seek support and comfort from another SAR family during the period of the missions.

A FINAL SEASON

I have always heard that older athletes want just "one more season." I am experiencing the same thing. I perceive my career is winding down, yet I want one more season, a final rescue to top them all

Well, I guess in a sense I have come full circle. I learned about life through the Red River Gorge Experience, and have grown old in the Gorge. I can think of no other place I would rather be, but the pallid shadow of impending retirement is ever present. Many people spend a great part of their working career looking forward to the day they can look back on it. As they approach retirement, they keep looking back wondering what's gaining on them.

Oliver Wendell Holmes once said, "It is very grand to die in harness, but it is pleasant to have the tight straps unbuckled and the heavy collar lifted from the neck and shoulders."

I firmly believe that all the years of your life are less important than the life in your years. So is retirement, after all, so bitter. I have attained what few men have dared, leaving a legacy for the generations to follow. The words of Henry W. Longfellow come to mind, "Age is opportunity no less than youth itself, though in another dress." Yet it is hard to go, even as I contemplate the rapidly fleeting time and dread each passing day, which brings me closer to leaving this engaging land that has provided me with so much. A' Tout a' Heure.

The word "IF" is one of the most used words in our language. It is defined as, on the condition, whether, and so forth. IF I had not come to the Red River Gorge that long ago autumn day, I probably would never be in the rescue realm. IF I had not become so dedicated to the job and formed this exceptional bond with the land, I probably would be retired by now. IF I had never seen Sky Bridge and IF a cow had wings she could fly.

Sky Bridge made a deep and lasting impression upon my young mind. In fact, its fall became a condition of my retirement. I was so taken with this wonder in stone that I was moved to compose The Saga of an Arch, presented in the following pages. In this

epistle the reader will find a bond between the arch and mankind related in the imaginary words of Sky Bridge articulating. In this mythical discussion the arch laments the passing of it's time as do we all From a lofty perch on the dividing ridge between Parched Corn and Swift Creek overlooking the Red River, the arch observes man's inhumanity to man and a wide variety of social injustice down through the ages.

And now, for whatever it is worth, here is the SAGA OF AN ARCH.

SAGA OF AN ARCH

My name is Sky Bridge. I am, what is known in human jargon, as a ridge top arch. There are many neighboring arches around, which are similar, yet different from me. They are called today by diverse names and are formed in several ways. Some of the types of arches I have heard about are cave, pothole, buttress, fin, pillar, bridging and, of course, ridge top.

But I am getting ahead of my story.

I can vaguely remember the time of my birth. At the close of the Paleozoic Era (about 225 million years ago) this area was uplifted during the Appalachian Orogeny. The record thereafter was one of erosion. By Cretaceous time (about 100 million years ago), a peneplain had developed a subsequent uplift, during Tertian time, (less than 70 million years ago), resulted in a plateau of dendrite drainages with a maze of irregularly winding, narrow crested ridges and deep narrow valleys. The effects of erosion and mass wasting created geomorphic conditions, principally narrow sandstone ridges, particularly suitable for the formation of arches.

Just before my birth, I was a long narrow ridge overlooking a river on a divide between two smaller streams. Here I was subject to weathering, erosion and mass wasting. Slowly at first, than more rapidly small sandstone blocks, formed by weathering and wedging action of water, ice and roots penetrating along joints and bedding planes; were detached from the underside of the ridge and moved down slope by gravity. Erosional undermining of my less-resistant underlying strata also contributed to the detachment. I must not forget the wind. It seems as if the wind was always blowing, moving minute grains of sand in a scouring effect along my surface.

After an untold number of years, I had developed into a sort of shallow cave or what is known as a ROCKSHELTER. The one fine day erosion forced an opening to the opposite side of the ridge. Very tiny to be sure, but at last light was passing completely through the ridge. I had become a LIGHTHOUSE! I stayed in this stage for many years while the forces of differential weathering enlarged the opening.

I cannot recall the exact time I passed from a lighthouse to an ARCH. The change was gradual and almost imperceptible, but I could feel a slight wearing away of my surface, but did not feel any significant loss of strength. Oh, it was great to be young, glorying in my strength at holding aloft an enormous span of rock above, in a configuration that would later be copied by man to hold large masses by the compression principle --what is known as an arch.

For what seems a long time after this I gradually began to feel a wearing away and weakening of my surface. It was sometime during this period that I became an object of awe and wonder to the first humans I ever met. To these people, now known as the ancient or early man, I was a part of them, sharing a common spirit. I can remember ceremonies under the curve of my arch. At this time, I took no particular notice, but in retrospect, I note these early people appeared to have a great respect for the land. The land and the ancients were one, each dependent upon the other.

Then came a time when I was alone again. The ancients had disappeared and I watched over a valley devoid of human fife. In the meantime, my surface was still flaking, scoured by the wind, water and temperature changes. I guess by now I would be considered a mature arch.

I observed over the valley and noted the Indians came again. The number who visited me continued to grow over the years, and many began to live here the year round. I remember when they started planting small plots of squash, sunflowers and goosefoot and asking me for a bountiful crop. Then the first members of the white race appeared upon my domain, and I witnessed my first major conflict between humans.

Something called War.

The Indians disappeared again, and I began to see small clearings or farms scattered sparsely around the area. Then something started to happen which I could not understand. The stately forest around me commenced to fall and there were many people, some with long sharp limber objects, who caused this fall. What noise these trees made as they crashed to the ground! The river below floated the logs out, and on almost every stream of any size a dam was constructed to hold back the water until sufficient volume was available to float the logs down to the river. Later, I witnessed the building of roads, and than one of the strangest sights I had every seen: That of a huffing, puffing, steel apparition on tracks that removed the logs and hauled them away.

I began to see more white settlers and their farms were scattered loosely over the area. Sometime during this period I started to receive visitors. Someone called me the BIG LIGHTHOUSE and this name stuck for a period. Later I was called SKY BRIDGE. I like the name and it has endured to this day. During this time I extolled in my slender graceful lines, and the image I must have portrayed from the valley floor! I was receiving thousands of visitors and was glad for the company.

After so many years of being exposed to the elements, I am aging. Millions of visitors have tramped across my spine loosening tiny grains of sand that gradually go deeper and deeper. Many thoughtless humans have carved their names or initials deep into my surface and on practically every vacant spot, thus hastening my demise. In fact, I believe I have suffered the loss of more surface material during the past 50 years than I have in the previous 5000 years.

I have grown old and am in the winter of my life. The constant stream of visitors is welcome, but I have become tired of the traffic. I have seen so many people who toss their trash carelessly about my surface. Some have even sprayed paint on me. Then a cleanup crew tries to remove the paint and in the process takes part of my surface with it. I can ill afford the loss at this stage of my life. Other people get close to my edge and plunge to the rocks below. I have heard it said I should be fenced on each edge of my spine. I shudder to think what would happen if postholes were drilled into my already weakened surface.

A few rare times I am alone with my memories. But they are magnificent memories. I remember the great plateau, the age-long sculpturing of my form, and the first people who came to visit me. I remember glorying in my youth, and what a fine figure I was at

that time. I remember how I was once an object of worship, held in awe and wonder, and now how people think nothing of cutting deeply into my surface, tossing trash or spraying paint. Such hurt and humiliation!

During my final time, I can only hope that people will once again respect the land. If you are walking across my spine, consider all the arches, and look upon our ageless struggle with the elements and do not hasten our fall. Please do not desecrate our surface with trash, carving and spray paint. I understand you are probably reaching out with an unconscious quest for immortality, but don't be deceived. All things must pass. We all have our moments; the spring, summer, autumn and winter of our lives.

So here I am, overlooking the valley below and the Red River. I am told that rivers sometimes rejuvenate themselves and become young again. I sometimes wish this could happen to me.

I dimly remember, someone saying one windy day from the top of my spine, some word over which I have often pondered. I believe he called it a Psalm and it goes something like this: "As for man, his days are as grass; as a flower of the field, so he flourisheth. For the wind passeth over it, and it is gone; and the place thereof shall know it no more."

Is this all there is for man? Will it be thus for me?

I wonder.

SOCIAL PROBLEMS IN THE ENVIRONS

Each time I hike to Sky Bridge, I an awestruck by the classic beauty and grandeur of this incredible work of nature. Nothing can prepare one for the experience of seeing such a unique feature firsthand. This freestanding span of stone, set against the backdrop of cliff -studded valleys of sheer palisade walls, leaves no doubt why it is the most famous arch in the eastern United States.

At the same time, as I stand on this magnanimous backbone, I am filled with anger and disgust. Chiseled into every reachable square inch of its graceful sandstone form is the graffiti of the multitudes who have visited over the years.

This brings to mind the lunatic who struck Michelangelo's Pieta with a sledgehammer several times in the center of the Vatican before a horrified crowd subdued him. Months of painstaking work restored the Pieta to near its original beauty. Unfortunately, no such option exists for Sky Bridge. Abrading out the deeply etched initials, names and dates would only remove that much more sandstone surface and probably would only serve to prepare a clean slate for a new wave of narcissistic defacement.

What can be done to stop this senseless outreaching for immortality? To date, remoteness is the only agent effective in protecting these awe evoking phenomenon. It may already be too late to do much for Sky Bridge, hut there are other arches that are at this time kept a distance from both the indiscriminate forces of progress and the thoughtless acts of vandals.

What manner of person defaces such ageless treasures? What social ills or injustice await the nearing generations if we destroy our natural environment? A study of ancient history relates that 19 of 21 civilizations perished from the face of the earth because of an inability to learn an existence cannot be maintained without the conservation of all our natural resources. To insure this nation will not be the 20th or so to perish, we must take positive steps now not to destroy our environment and those who habitat it. Destroy any species and you destroy a historical monument older by far than any works of man.

Until perceptions change and people find better ways of dealing with our environs, the list of endangered species will, at least implicitly, include humans.

The reader may be wondering if I am diverging from the sociology of SAR, so rest assured that I am still on track. Since mostly all SAR missions are in the environs, we have a duty to protect natural features from impairment by the mission. This includes unnecessary clearing of brush, harm to T&E species, damage to natural features, and by selecting evacuation routes along the path of least resistance.

Also, the natural features of the Gorge are the attraction to thousands of visitors. Unfortunately, many visitors have, what appears to be, an unconscious reaching out for eternal life in the form of cutting names and initials or spray painting some of the conspicuous features of this great land. The historic Nada Tunnel is a good example. Thoughtless or uncaring visitors have spray painted names and initials along most of the interior of the 800 feet long tunnel. Long known as the gateway to the Red River Gorge, the graffiti is the first thing to greet guests to the area. Not only has the Nada Tunnel suffered this disrespect and indignity, but even the exquisite sandstone surface of the cliffs close to the road, have not been spared. The first time visitor, expecting a pristine land, is in for a surprise when his eyes are directed the multitude collection of wall scrawl.

Even some of the cliffs in the remote environs reveal the stamp of various names and initials cut deeply into the sandstone surface. Some carving has taken place near the extreme edge of the cliffs and has been the impetus to several SAR missions.

On one particular mission, the victim was carving his name in a place very difficult to reach but in a spot where no other names existed, a perfect place to grasp a measure of immortality. The subject negotiated a narrow semblance of a ledge to a large smooth wall The subject reached out to start his inscription, slipped and fell about 30 feet. He was apparently only minor injured from the fall, but received a cut on the leg when he fell on the open knife

blade which he had been using in an attempt to cut into the rock. A social injustice becomes justice.

There appears to be no way to measure the social injustice of the acts of vandalism, or the social ills of those who commit them. Of course cutting names, dates and initials into rocks or trees has been practiced since man learned to write his name. In earlier times, this mark of identification was used for practical reasons. Now it has reached runaway proportions, bringing into the natural areas the same social problems that characterize cities.

A REVIEW OF SAFETY AND RISK FACTORS

A person standing on the North Pole has no place to go except south. No matter in which direction he turns, when he steps forward he can only walk south. The feeling of having only one direction to go may not be a new one in some of our lives. However, in any direction we advance, we should plan for safety as far as possible. Thus safety will become an absolute force, not an opposing one. The ancient Chinese Bah Kua or the symbol of Yang and Yin, unfold the balance between good and evil, positive and negative as well as all the other opposites.

Admiral Richard Byrd, the famous polar explorer, once related: "In all my travels and adventures in the interest of science and discovery, I have never taken an `unnecessary risk.' Only the best and safest equipment was selected for planes and ships. Everything was made safe that could be made safe. By careful planning and by taking no unnecessary chances, my men and I have lived to enjoy the hazards and thrills of adventure and discovery. We found adventure only by planning for safety as far as possible.

The term "Safety First" asks only for the good adventure instead of the bad. An accident is a bad adventure. The slogan asks for a worthwhile goal that gives purpose to risk. An accident is usually meaningless. It asks for accomplishment and success instead of waste and failure. An accident is a failure.

People sometimes seem to be divided into two major groups as related to safety, the nearsighted and the farsighted. The nearsighted person looks upon safety as too tedious and boring, or as a job which is never done. The farsighted, knowing that safety is a vital part of success, sees in the same task a means to his goal.

An old Chinese philosopher, Lao-Tzu, epitomized the situation in a few words: " A journey of a thousand miles begins with a single step." The true safety-minded person takes that first step-and keeps on going.

The safety movement has never advocated safety as the number one objective in life.
It has never opposed adventure, which along with discovery, is the very essence of life. Rather it asks for planning, thought and a safe approach to work and play situations. It asks for training and a good safety attitude.

Yet accidents still happen. They happen to the untrained, the inexperienced, to those who think an accident cannot happen to them, and the ones who consider accidents as a matter of luck or fate. Mishaps can come to everyone who may be unprepared for them. Carelessness and overconfidence are usually more hazardous than deliberate accepted risks. Most accidents are caused by mistakes, which could have been avoided.

To make the assumption the rescue team plunges into a situation with a reckless disregard for personal safety in order to save someone in distress is inaccurate. There are many risks in any SAR operation, but especially in the high cliff' realm. Risks are an inherent part of SAR, but they are never taken lightly. Everything that can be made safe is executed before the operation begins. This is known as "controlled risks." Immediately upon arrival of an accident scene, an evaluation is made of the risk factors that can be confirmed at the time. Steps are taken to minimize or abate t h e risks prior to commencing the m cue operation. While each team member is skilled is his specialty, if necessity dictates he can take over any other team member's job. The circle of completeness of the Bah Kua.

Even being a "Good Samaritan" is not without risk. In legal theory, the bystander is safe as long as he or she does absolutely nothing. But as soon as steps are taken to help, immunity for failure to act is removed. If a bystander decides to act as a "Good Samaritan" and chooses to intervene, he or she will be liable to the victim if rescue actions were unreasonable, and indeed aggravated the plight of the victim.

As long as nothing is done to worsen the situation, a "Good Samaritan" can abandon the rescue effort and leave the scene. However, at some point someone who intervenes is considered to have assumed a legal duty to act. This point is still unclear in law. The old common law still protects a rescuer from liability for trespass if the individual uses others' goods to save lives or protect property. For example, a "Good Samaritan" can break into a garage and seize an axe to save a stranger trapped in a burning car.

Another exception occurs when a person creates a situation placing another in danger. A negligent motorist who causes an accident involving injuries is liable if he or she does not provide assistance.

In some circumstances, a person is assumed to have a duty to assist because of the nature of employment. Police and paid fireman are required to assist in an emergency. In general, a "Good Samaritan" is not paid for rescuing people in danger.

The biblical parable of the "Good Samaritan" is used to teach the virtue of helping someone in need. Is this virtue common under our legal system? How would the priest and Levite be treated in our courts for their unwillingness to assist a fellow traveler on the Jericho Road?

As a general principle, common law does not require a bystander to help someone in peril --the priest and the Levite would not be liable for failing to assist the stranger. However, some exceptions exist where failure to act could result in liability. A so-called "special relationship" may give rise to a duty to assist. An example would be an employer may be obligated to assist his employee injured at work and innkeepers must aid their guests.

Liability exists where there is negligence. Negligence is an unintentional action, which causes harm to another. There are four elements of negligence: (1) Duty or Standard, (2) Breach of duty, (3) Causation, (4) Actual loss or harm. If any one of these is not present, the result would be the dismissal of a claim of liability.

If liability is determined by the court and a judgment rendered it will be on the basis of Comparative Negligence which has replaced the historic Contributory Negligence. By this method the amount of wrongdoing of the plaintiff is compared to that of the agency. If a judgment is established, and it is determined the plaintiff is 2/3rds responsible and the agency 1/3, the settlement will be 1/3 of the total amount stipulated in the judgment, because the plaintiff is 2/3 censurable.

An old adage chronicles, "The two greatest adventures a person will every experience is birth and death." How long a span we have between these two events may depend to a certain extent upon our attitudes and how well we follow established safety principles.

Risk and hazard will always be present in our lives. If we are to live and work, we will experience some element of danger. However, danger can be mastered by people of mature judgment who believe with Shakespeare that, "Out of this nettle danger, we pluck this flower, safety."

FOREST SERVICE SAR POLICY

"There are always possibilities."
-Star Trek-

Search and Rescue is covered in the FSM 1599 SEARCH AND RESCUE, which reads: The Forest Service recognizes its public duty to render assistance in cases involving persons lost, seriously ill, injured or deceased and transport from National Forest to a point where victim may be received by local authorities.

Under AUTHORITY of the same section authorizes the Forest Service to incur Necessary expenses in search and rescue operations. This statute imposes no duty, the breach of which would be actionable at law, on the Forest Service to search for and rescue persons on the National Forest.

Under POLICY of the same section the guidance is that the Forest Service takes a temporary lead role in any search and rescue emergency in which immediate and quick response will reduce suffering and save lives. The concept of closest forces must be used and the lead role maintained only until the predetermined local responsible authority is available to assume its leadership. After transferring the leadership role, the Forest Service shall assume a supportive role and provide assistance to the fullest extent possible.

Therein lies the problem: There is no predetermined local authority! The public looks to the Forest Service for help in emergency situations. Not only the public, but the Powell, Menifee and Wolfe County Sheriffs Department, Kentucky State Police and Natural Bridge State Park. None of these agencies have the personnel and specialized equipment required to pluck the dead or injured from the high cliffs of the Gorge. Their first act is to call the Red River Gorge Mountain Rescue Team.

And rightly so. The team has accomplished over 1500 search and rescue missions. These range from high cliff to chairlift rescues and just about everything in between. They have removed dogs from cracks and crevices; children from old abandoned hand dug wells and once even retrieved a cell phone from the unsavory vault of an outdoor toilet. It was returned to the thankful owners.

The Red River Gorge Mountain Rescue Team will carry on as before until there is no longer a need for their services.

UNPREDICTABLE RISK

"When shall we three meet again in thunder, lightning, or in rain?"
-Shakespeare-

Throughout this missive substantial reference has been made to risk and risk taking, as well as the different types of risk. What can be controlled or mitigated is done at the beginning of the mission. However, there are risks that are uncertain and cannot be controlled in the least. Such a risk is nature's fury in the form of storms and especially deadly lightning. Such awesome displays of fight are ghastly around high cliffs. There is nothing one can do when caught on the cliffs in a thunderstorm except hope and pray.

It was a dark stormy night. Lightning danced across the night sky flashing the tense faces of the rescue team as they guided the stokes litter up the face of a sheer cliff wall High cliff rescue, while always dangerous, is intensified during a thunderstorm due to all the metal components of the system attracting the lightning bolts. While I have never experienced lightning striking a rescue configuration, I have seen it too close for comfort. In the above incident I observed a display of lightning which appeared to ring around the team and litter in a startling scene of heaven and hell combined. The helmets of the team members appeared as crown of light to the apparition backdrop of the rising fog half shrouding the entire rescue scene. For a moment I was transfigured by this phenomenon to such an extent that I almost stopped the raise monetarily, not believing what my eyes perceived.

Why take such risk? The National Search and Rescue Association has a motto: "So That Others Might Live." It is, however, more than that. All individuals need satisfying group participation, since there are basic psychological needs, which can be fulfilled only in a social situation. The development of a sense of self, the famous "looking-glass" self of the sociologist, presupposes a group of people from whom the individual sees himself reflected and against whose reactions he tests himself. This is the glue that holds a rescue team together. A unity and sense of belonging are dynamic forces to the individual team member, along with the fact that are helping someone in need. With the knowledge they are unique, a special kind of team doing a highly skilled task, creates a powerful group bond

Being a part of group life starts at the moment of birth. Much of what happens to an individual for the rest of the lifespan happens in groups of one sort or another. The rescue team is a group of highly motivated individuals from different walks of life who have chosen to help others. They are a small group who depend eminently upon each. While the individual jobs are specialized, each team member must he prepared to take over another team members job on a momentary notice. Such interdependence has created a strong social bond, and fostered a consequential relationship to the Red River Gorge that is somewhat akin to devotion.

I have experienced only two rescues as a result of lightning striking a person. One of these happened near Sky Bridge. Two young men had sought sanctuary from a vicious thunderstorm in a rock shelter near the bridge. Lightning entered the shelter and stuck both occupants. The entry of the strike appeared almost imperceptible while the exit was a large bum area. Both victims were transported to a hospital. The second event was at Indian Stairway where another young man was standing on the cliff face watching an approaching storm. He was electrified and rendered unconscious for a period of time, but survived the strike. According to his version, he experienced a tingling sensation and his hair seemed to stand on end just before he was struck. Again there were bums, but no known lasting effects. His friends indicated he was daring the lightning to touch him.

Here we have two extremes: one seeking shelter from lightning, the other daring to inveigle nature. The Bah Kua is said to prove the identity of contraries. Aristotle's golden mean of a straight line between two extremes, contrasts with this symbol of no straight fines, and all in a circle of completeness. The ancient Chinese philosophy, Taoism brings forth the belief that nature is to be befriended. In fact, it was taught that through a mystical union with the Tao (nature) one could transcend nature and even life and death. So, in the example of lightning do we find a vestige of Yang and Yin?

Alan Watts, in Nature, Man and Woman, contrasts the western

approach to nature (nature is to be conquered, defined and made subject to technology) with the eastern approach (nature is an organic whole in which man is fully included and feels at home).

Ecological problems are essentially psychological and sociological ones, but there appear to be no simple solutions. If we cannot learn from the past, then man himself, may become the endangered species.

Vine Deloria, Jr., in his book We talk, You listen, argued the only way out of the effects that threaten humanity today would be for man to adopt the Indian's ways of relating to nature.

The typical western approach is not the way the rescue team views the Red River Gorge. In fact, some have been heard to remark they work in some of the most spectacular scenery in the nation. Caring for the land is evinced in the way rescuers remove the victim, by going around obstacles rather then trying to clear them out of the way. For example, a person is sent ahead to scout the evacuation route and guide the litter bearers in the most achievable way. This is in sharp contrast to cutting a path in the direction you want to go. The same goes with refuse from the mission. Nothing is left behind.

"He who knows not and knows not that he knows not, is a fool, shun him;
He who knows not, and knows that he knows not, is a child, teach him.
He who knows, and knows not that he knows, is asleep, wake him.
He who knows, and knows that he knows, is wise, follow him."

-Persian Proverb-

The Rescue team became over time, a highly trained, well motivated, contingent that was featured on several television programs including PM Magazine, a Lexington based operation, of the national syndicated show. A representative of PM magazine heard about the team and decided to propose the story to give credit for the rescue team's work in the Red River Gorge. A mock rescue was staged, that had bystanders wondering if it were the real thing.

This was during the tenure of the all Forest Service volunteer team. As I have so often stated, this was the ultimate assemblage in teamwork and social interaction with the victim. By this time the reader may be wondering? Who were these supermen and where are they now? I look out on the mythical corral at the empty saddles with imaginary emblazon names and wonder where all the years have gone!

Kendal Culbertson -- A Supervisory Law Enforcement Officer for the north Zone. Honored with the National Law Enforcement Officer of the year award, he is still with the team accumulating over 23 years of service. An absolute master at strategy on how to remove victims from the precipitous cliff wall

Johnny Faulkner --Resigned from the team several years ago. Too much blood, pain and suffering was his reason. This resignation came as a shock and much sorrow. Johnny, the wizard of the ropes,

was giving up search and rescue! His feats on the rescues were legendary and he is still missed, particularly in complex rescue situations. He is still with the Forest Service in the Archaeology realm.

Phil Koontz - Transferred north to another forest as a Law Enforcement Officer. I have lost contact with him over the years, but understand he is doing well His dedication to the cause and empathy for the victim made him a valuable member of the team.

Jack Courtney --Transferred south to Texas and still with the Forest Service. Jack was a big man, exceptionally strong and could still perform near miraculous aerobics on the high cliffs. A difficult saddle to fill.

Gary Hawkins--Transferred to Arkansas as a Recreation Manager. I understand he will soon be in the same capacity at the Land Between the Lakes in Kentucky soon. I look forward to a reunion. He was always willing to respond to a call day or night and readily accepted the most difficult challenge. His victim empathy was peerless.

Morris Drake - He left the Forest Service at the end of a temporary appointment, and is at present the owner of a computer business. He was the comic of the team. Highly educated, he had an answer for everything and kept up the team's spirit no matter how arduous or complicated the task.

As for me, I'm still here. A little older and I hope wiser. I did not retire after my 1300th rescue as I vowed on that long ago late autumn day. I guess I will wait for Sky Bridge to fall, the other retirement alternative.

My thoughts go back to the early 1960's when the rescue team consisted of whomever I could find to go with me. Gradually, with the few trained volunteers as a nucleus, the Red River Gorge Rescue came into being out of necessity with ever increasing falls from high cliffs becoming a common occurrence. By the time the team embodied all Forest Service volunteers, there was an average of about 65 rescues each year. Most of them, falls from high cliffs.

As with all things, this dream team faded into obscurity a few years later due to attrition. Yet, I longed for one more season with the team

unaltered once again, knowing full well it is was impossible. There was only one thing left to do. Rebuild the team with new people, but keep the traditions established by the old one. It was a seemingly monumental task to take a new group and tell them they were a high cliff rescue crew, especially after such a unique team had dispersed and gone their separate ways.

Time has a way of dimming memories. I was fortunate in my choice of volunteers who after a period, and with the able expertise of Kendal, became a solid entity, accepting the old traditions and performing admirable. The volunteers are recognized in the acknowledgements section.

Events appear to have come full circle. Here I am in the twilight of my career and the volunteer team is shrinking again! We will start a modern training program for neoteric members come spring. It is wrong, of course, to anticipate the same members to stay year after year. Family considerations, loss of vigor, and just plain wearing out are taken into account. Not to mention the high risk or injury or death. I am thankful for all the volunteers who have taken such risks down through the past legion of years. In my humble insignificance, I can only testify that each and every one of the volunteers has sacrificed much so that "others might five."

Facing the ghostly specter of impending retirement, I look beyond the Red River Gorge and see...Nothing! How does a person reach this state of mind? How may one explain a love of the land so complete it supplied everything I every needed or wanted. I honestly don't know how this happened, but it was gradual and almost imperceptible over a long period of time. I have spent most of my lifetime in this unique place. Regrets? None. Had I the opportunity to live my life over again, I would do the same thing.

It has been over 40 years since I first gazed over the spiny prominences of the Red River Gorge and told myself this is where I belong. I sometimes retreat into my memories. But they are magnificent memories. I remember the Honor Awards Ceremony at Washington, D.C., the Presidential Citation from Ronald Reagan, the Congressman's Award of Merit, the page in the Congressional Record, and many local honors. I especially remember the over 1500 Search and Rescue missions, some with happy endings, but far too many tragedies.

The Gorge too, received many honors. It 1974 it was designated a National Geological Area, in 1975, a National Natural Landmark, and in 1985 a Wilderness Area. I stood by and marveled as proud of the Gorge as of my own honors. Of course I played my own tiny part in the designations.

BEYOND THE RED RIVER GORGE! How many times have I considered this over the past many years. Always with a dread that I must someday leave this special place that has provided me with myriad unique experiences over such a long span. It really gets to me. I know it is not good-bye, but it is farewell, A' Tout a' l' Heure, a French phrase meaning "I'll see you again." I must cling to that hope.

PREPLANNING

The shrill distance ringing of the telephone finally broke the deep sleep I glanced at the clock. 1:30 AM. I'm setting too old for this, I thought, even as my mind raced ahead with preplanning. I have learned over 45 years the importance of playing out a scenario in your mind prior to the actual rescue.

The professional voice of the dispatcher was feeding out the information into my
ear. Half Moon Rock again. My mind kicked into gear spewing out information from previous rescues. Suitable anchors scarce, overhang over cliff edge, jagged rock face and so on.

Arriving at Half Moon, I set to work analyzing the situation, while Kendal rappelled over to check on the victim. I have been here before and knew a raise system was needed. Anchors, as anticipated, were in short supply forcing me to rig a self-equalizer and run the haul line through Half Moon Arch. Edge rollers and clothing were used as rope protectors. Safety lines were rigged; and remembering my last experience here, added a load release knot to the raise system. All was ready and everything that could he made safe was made safe. Waiting now for word from Kendall to start the raise.

At Kendal's command we started the raise, which went well at first. Approaching the overhanging lip I began to manipulate the ropes in the hope I could negotiate the edge without major problems. It was not to be so. The litter stuck fast. I slowly and carefully manipulated the load release knot lowering a foot or so to free the jammed stretcher. Two rescuers were lowered to opposite ends of the litter and by pulling outwards at the same time as the raise, negotiated the lip in classic style.

This incident shows the value of preplanning. By recall, my memory played out some of the problems the team might encounter. For example, the Load Release Knot allows the litter to he safely lowered if an overhanging cliff edge is encountered during a raise. It is very difficult to tie after the fact.

It may also save packing in surplus equipment, but more importantly, adds an extra margin of safety. Of course this requires long experience but each team member should he aware of the value of obser^v^ation on rescue missions.

THE SAFETY RECORD

In writing about the safety record I am reminded of all the mythical "empty saddles" existing now only in the realms of my memory. I especially remember the all Forest Service team...here I go again!

The safety record of the team is astounding. In 45 years covering 1,653 rescue missions there was only one mishap to a team member that required hospitalization. There were, of course, a number of near misses. The controlled risk factor was the dominating action.

The injury occurred on a late night rescue at Chimney Rock to an experienced team member, a veteran of many late night sorties. While making his way down to a victim of a cliff fall, he failed to negotiate a ledge, dropped down and struck a tree root, fracturing an ankle. He waited in stoic silence until the original rescue had been completed and only then would he consent to he moved. He was carried out in a stokes basket, a completely strange experience for him who had carried out many victims this way. The ankle curtailed his SAR activities for weeks. But this amazing man had to be helping in some way, so he monitored the radio system giving advice and directions to rescue scenes as needed. His name is Click Castle, an outstanding paragon of the SAR profile.

Some near misses include

- Fall while negotiating a narrow ledge near half moon arch
- A near tragedy when team member slipped and almost went over cliff
- Nose struck cliff when rescuer slipped on wet moss while rappelling
- Copperhead struck and attached to toe of boot
- Member dropped carabineer and while retrieving almost touched a Copperhead
- Member was climbing Tower Rock when he came face to face with a rattlesnake
- Member fell while climbing. Belay held
- Member fell into river while carrying the litter over a narrow ledge
- Rescuer ran out of rope while rappelling to victim
- Rope sheath cut while rappelling
- Rescuers Gibbs ascender came loose while climbing up with litter

FINALE

"Every dog must have his day"
-Swift-

As this document has reached its finale, perhaps it is time to reminisce on the many SAR missions. I never really thought of sociology, until this article was requested. To a sociologist, this report is probably an exercise in futility. To the SAR reader, it hopefully will not be meaningless, but rather will be a foundation upon which sound decisions can be made concerning the sociology of SAR.

Nothing has been mentioned about dog rescue from cracks and crevices. I have always liked dogs and on many occasions incurred considerable risk in retrieval. What is the sociology of SAR as far as dogs are concerned? Certainly, some dog owners feel the dog is part of the family. To them, standing by and doing nothing is akin to refusing to rescue a child. I shall never forget "Sugar", a 13 year old, white Pekinese, partially blind, who stumbled through an overlook and fell over 100 feet.

The call came in as an unknown request for assistance. Arriving at the area. I encountered the frantic dog owner who reported that Sugar had fallen over the overlook. Taking stock of the situation. I decided to rappel over the cliff (how many times before) in an effort to locate the dog. Finding nothing on the various ledges, I continued on to the base of the cliff where I located Sugar. A quick examination indicated a broken pelvis and jaw. Even in obvious pain the dog tried to greet me and seemed happy someone had come. The problem now was how to best move her with these grievous injuries. Making her as comfortable as possible, I decided to walk down the slope to Red River (about a mile) with Sugar in my arms. The trip out was one in which I attempted to negotiate the steep, rugged terrain and still keep from jostling the little dog unnecessary. Through it all Sugar was stoic, bearing her pain with never an outcry. I delivered Sugar to her owner, who rushed her to the nearest Vet. Our brief sojourn left a lasting impression on me, and I was deeply disturbed to learn the little dog's injuries were so severe she had to be put to sleep. At least she died with her loved one and not on some rocky crag exposed to the elements. I take some comfort in that.

While all SAR missions are significant sometimes certain ones remain anamnesis. One such incident involved a child falling from a cliff. When the frantic parents calmed enough to advise me of the situation, I assembled my rescue gear and stepped cautiously over the edge as I have done so many times in the past. Carefully working my way down to the first ledge, I found the young child who appeared to be without a major injury! By this time additional help was arriving via the rope highway. The team members on top began to rig a 3 to 1 haul system, lowering a stokes litter, backboard and medical supplies. Meanwhile, I had been carrying on a dialogue with the young victim, calming his fears and reassurance of a speedy reunion with his parents.

The trip to the top was without incident. Emerging over the cliff edge, I was greeted by his grateful parents even as I heard the wailing siren of the approaching ambulance.

In that brief moment, I felt the sears lift from me and I was young again.

What is the social significance of the incidents of the aging dog and the young child? Possibly nothing or maybe, just a paradoxical of a boy and a dog.

SAR members must constantly remind themselves to avoid unrealistic expectations imposed by themselves or by society. We cannot save the world. Possibly we can help only our small piece of it. Be the best of whatever you are. The SAR motto "So That Others Might Live", sums up the social aspect of SAR.

I have heard, somewhere, that there are OLD rescuers and BOLD rescuers. But there are no OLD/BOLD rescuers. No attempt to analyze this in relationship to SAR sociology would he justified.

It is my earnest hope that in reading this article you have learned a little about SAR in the Red River Gorge. Not only the SAR, but the social relations between the rescuer, victim, relatives and media. Certainly this is not intended to be a "how to" theme, since social relations are constantly changing. Rather, it is hoped the reader may gain some insight into understanding social goals as they apply to the SAR mission.

There is a old truism stating, "The only thing constant is change." I leave you with that final thought.

Good Luck!

ACKNOWLEDGMENTS

A special debt of gratitude is owed to all the many volunteers who have assisted the Red River Gorge Rescue Team all these years. While each and every one is deserving of special recognition, there occasionally comes forth individuals who have really made the team click. One such individual is Alan Cornette, who was a regular on the team for many years until advancing age intervened. Al is an artist who lives at Slade, KY and was in an ideal location for responding to Gorge emergencies. I have seem him perform some amazing feats on the ropes and his caring attitude toward the victim was peerless. Other outstanding individuals include:

William "Grizzly" Cloyd, a bear of a man, who joined the team in 1993 and is still active. Grizzly keeps both victim and team entertained with his witticism, which helped the long treks out seem a little shorter. For a big man, he moves with ease and grace and is always willing to shoulder (as well he might) the heavy tasks. In spite of his sometimes shenanigans (such as hanging on to the stretcher in order to get back up a cliff face) he has provided an invaluable service to the victim and team. I well remember a rescue on half-moon rock where we were moving the stretcher up a series of small cliff ledges. Grizzly had been wondering how he was going to get back up the cliff ledge at one particular point. When the stretcher started up, he had an inspiration. He simply latched on the litter and (unknown to me) allowed the team to pull both him and the litter up. Since I have made numerous rescues in this location, when the litter progress came to an abrupt halt, I looked around expecting the stretcher was hung or some type of equipment failure. Little did I realize there was 270 pounds of Grizzly attached to the litter. His comments on body bags are best left unsaid.

James Cloyd (son of Grizzly) started as a greenhorn, but through diligent training and experience has become the best rescue person since Johnny Faulkner. In many respects he rivals Johnny. I have watched him perform astounding search and rescue feats and he has deep empathy for the victims, a fine young man and a volunteer since 1993.

Ken Munday has been with the team since 1985. A highly skilled EMT as well as a very competent SAR person, he has certainly seen his share of victim pain and suffering. He has always been a quick responder bringing a vast amount of knowledge and skill to the scene over his many years of dedicated service.

Eddie Barnes, a former Deputy Sheriff', has served with distinction since 1992 is rarely active. A highly skilled EMT, he has established time and time again a special rapport with injured victims. His social interpersonal relationship with the victim, relatives and friends is superb. Yes, he finally learned to tie the Bowline Knot

Mike Tipton, a school counselor, is no longer active. However, it is fitting and proper that he given his just due for past service. He was a dynamic catalyst to the team when attrition was at its peak

Click Castle, a volunteer, served with honor. He was called upon time and time again for response to emergencies. His calm countenance and booming voice was a trademark in the rescue community. He has retired from SAR.

Jim Porter, a volunteer, was always an excellent source of knowledge. He was constantly striving to improve the rescue techniques, and devised a cart pulled by an ATV with all attachments for the safe transporting of the victim in a stokes litter. A wonderful addition saving countless hours of carrying the stokes.

Daniel Porter. a volunteer, driver of the ATV and a valuable roustabout Young, vigorous and strong, he proved his worth on many missions.
Richard Beshears, a volunteer, he was an absolute master of the ropes, performing some amazing feats while orchestrating a raise or lower configuration. He is now retired.

J.L. Bowen, a volunteer, took to the training like a duck to water, and emerged as one of the finest high cliff rescuers on the team. No longer active on the cliffs, but is in command of the EMS in Powell County.

Mike Kelso, a Deputy Sheriff, has been a part of the team for several years. An accomplished EMT, he has the ability to quickly and accurately access a victims condition. In the Australian rappel incident he undoubting saved the life of the casualty.

There were many more who served: Tom Martin, Gerald Goldy, Gary Bowen, Alan Culbertson, just to name a few. They all played their part, lived their hour and left behind many unblemished memories of their service
Too many empty saddles!

APPENDIX

"No wise man ever wished to be younger"

-Swift-

Following are a few unusual SAR missions the reader may find of interest:
Three accidents in the span of an hour one Saturday night left the Red River Gorge Mountain Rescue Team scattered throughout the gorge attending to the victims. To complicate matters a significant rainfall was occurring rendering the cliff faces slick and hazardous.

The first rescue call came at 7:30 p.m., when a young man fell over 165 feet from a cliff off Chimney Rock road. While the team was engaged in this accident, another call came at 8:00 p.m. reporting a fall at Indian Stairway. Dividing the team was not the acceptable solution, but there was no choice. Four team members responded to Indian Stairway, and three continued the original rescue. Before the team could reach Indian Stairway, a third call advised of a fall near Pinch-Em-Tight gap. The team split again, two continuing on, and two diverting to the gap.

Conditions were unbelievable, the rain and fog cut visibility, soaked rescue gear and cadre, as well as rendering the cliffs even more dangerous. Worse yet, the limited amount of SAR gear had been divided three ways leaving each sub team a bare minimal. Volunteers at each scene assisted team members immeasurably, especially in the long pack out.

The results of the rescue near Chimney Rock – concussion, back injuries, probable internal injuries. Fell 165 feet.

Indian Stairway - cervical spine, fracture ribs and a probable punctured lung, and a broken leg. Fell 100 feet.

Pinch-em-Tight Gap - broken leg, multiple bruises and contusions. Fell 40 feet.
Although as many as four accidents have occurred in the Red River Gorge during one day, this marks the first time three accidents have happened almost simultaneously.

The headlines read: **FOUR FALLS IN RED RIVER GORGE REQUIRE RESCUE TEAM EFFORTS.** One weekend, four separate falls kept the team busy. The first call was at 2:30 a.m. on Saturday when a young male subject fell from Moonshiners Arch while wandering around without a light. He suffered a back injury and several broken ribs.

The second call came at 3:00 p.m. the same days when a young male fell about 90 feet while rock climbing in the Tight Hollow area. Internal injury, fractured ribs and a compressed vertebra.

The third call came Sunday morning at 10:30 a.m. A middle age male subject was suddenly taken ill (apparently appendicitis attack) on Chimney Top creek and had to be carried out in stokes litter about two miles.

The fourth call, and the most serious, occurred around 3:30 p.m. when a young female subject fell 75 feet near Hole-in-the wall, in the Clifty Creek area. She was apparently squatted and urinating on the edge of the cliff when she lost her balance and fell. She suffered internal injuries, compressed vertebra, broken leg and ankle.

Two teenagers (male and female) fell 80 from cliff near Natural Bridge. Female's foot slipped into a leaf-covered crevice and as she started falling, male reached to grab her and both went over the cliff edge. Female suffered serious internal injuries, male suffered broken jaw and multiple lacerations.

A 54 year old woman fell about 120 feet to her death at Sky Bridge. She strayed too close to the edge and lost her footing. This was her second trip to the arch on this day.

A young female, sleeping at the edge of Half Moon Rock rolls of the cliff. She plunges close to 100 feet, suffering fractured ribs, internal injuries and a concussion. But she survives.

A young male is sleeping on the edge of cliff. A sleepy turn and over he tumbled, falling about 35 to a ledge. Suffered a dislocated shoulder.

Another young male fell about 100 feet in the Indian Stairway area after he chased a roll of toilet paper over the edge of cliff. He sustained a broken collar bone and multiple bruises and contusions.

The list goes on and on. These are just a few of the more dramatic cases. They do not include people who get lost, capsize their canoes, or suffer lesser injuries. The incidents were selected randomly from the files.

If I live to be a hundred, I shall never forget a night on Chimney Rock where I was answering a call concerning a victim who had rolled over the cliff in his sleeping bag. When I leaned over the edge and called, I was surprised to receive an answer. On a ledge about 30 feet below the rim, I spotted a sleeping bag. Telling the victim not to move. I assembled my rescue gear and prepared for the descent over the cliff.

The rope journey down went well and in a minute or so, I was with the victim. I questioned him concerning what injury he may have and he replied he did not know. He was alert and conscious and I really could not find anything out of order. Taking no chances, I called for a backboard and cervical collar. Hawkins joined me on the ledge while other team members began to rig the 3 to I rescue haul system. It was a smooth operation and the top was quickly gained. Several bystanders were standing around watching and I requested their help in packing out the victim. In short order we were at the parking lot. The victim requested I loosen the straps on the litter. I complied by opening the straps in preparation for loading in the ambulance when it arrived. I had turned my attention to other matters, when I heard the victim say, "There's my car." Whereupon he got out of the litter, unlocked his car and with a cheerful, "Thanks Fellows," drove off. Needless to say I was dumbfounded. He had gotten a free ride to his car! He probably has many a chuckle as he recalls the incident from time to time. As for me, I live and learn.

Outside of the dying lady with whom I failed to establish social contact, the most compunctious incident was the one where a 2 year old children drown in the upper Red River and the father insisted on carrying out the infant in his arms with no help.

Another one was at Rainbow point where several young people were camping. Two wandered away from the group and fell about 165 feet. One was found dead face down on the rock and the other lying a short distance away and still alive.

The most frightening rescue occurred on 10/10/98. While transporting a victim over a very narrow ledge near Half Moon Rock, one of the rescuers nearly fell from a 100 foot cliff when he lost his balance and tumbled backward. He landed on his back and caught a tree at the edge of the cliff. This was the closest call for any member of the RRGMRT since it's origin in 1968.

While I have always taken an exorbitant pride in the accomplishments of the team members, an incident occurred on 06/15/97, which enhanced this outlook further. At 5:30 that morning I was notified that a young man had fallen about 200 feet from Eagles Peak. Three other team members, besides myself, responded there were Kendal (always) Grizzly and James Cloyd and Richard Brashears. Arriving in the area the victim was found on a narrow ledge about 75 feet above the ground. It was decided that Kendal, James and Richard would go to the top in an attempt to rappel down to the casualty. Grizzly and I would stay on the bottom. They were unable to reach him on the first attempt since the rope was only 165 feet in length. Obtaining a second rope, they rappelled to the first ledge, anchored the second rope and were able to reach the victim. The first person on the ledge was Kendal who observed the victim hanging on to a small bush with one hand and was about to fall. Unable to reach him, Kendal improvised a fanny pack with a loop in the belt, which he secured over the victims wrist just as he fell.

Holding on to a tree with one hand, the fanny pack with the other, Kendal managed to clasp on until James and Richard reached him. Together they pulled the man to safety. He was placed in the stokes with James guiding the litter down with the victim, and Kendal managing the lower system. When James and the litter touched bottom, Grizzly and I, along with James and four bystanders maneuvered the litter down the steep slopes to the river, where the victim was placed in a boat for the one mile trip down stream to the waiting ambulance. Words cannot describe the skill and courage of James Cloyd on the cliff face as he guided the litter over the precipitous terrain, supported by a few thin ropes. An admirable young man who is rapidly becoming a second Johnny Faulkner. I know that Grizzly must be as proud as I am. Later, Kendal received the U.S. Forest Service Law Enforcement Officer of the Year award for this rescue, among other things. My cup runneth over!

Two Chair Lift failures at Natural Bridge State Park (08/08/92 and 09/01/97) provided the Team with a different type of rescue. That of removing stranded visitors from the incapacitated chairlift. Using ropes, seat harness, and cliff rescue techniques, the Team was equal to this task. An elderly foreign couple who could not speak English had to be placed into a stokes litter from the chair seat and lowered down, reminiscence of a cliff rescue. All in all over 22 visitors were removed in the first operation and 16 in the latter.

I see no mention has been made of the young lady with the beautiful long hair who was rappelling from Half-moon rock when her hair became entangled in the figure 8 rappelling device. She managed to halt her descent but as the hair, caught in the device had pulled her head uncomfortably forward; she could not take the pressure off the 8 ring for risk of falling. Fortunately, she was near a small nodule on the cliff, which her toes could beady grip providing a temporary relief. She had been in this position for some time when I arrived. Needless to say, she was not in the best of moods. Rappelling down alongside her, I attached a pick-off strap to her harness, whipped out my knife and in seconds, part of her long tresses were history. When we reached the bottom of the cliff, I had never heard so many foul phrases delivered out of such a fair mouth.

I could go on and on but it would serve no useful purpose except to reminisce and that is not always a good thing. Shelly said: "We look before and after, and pine for what is not." An accounting of these incidents is simply for the purpose of making visitors aware that the Red River Gorge can be a place of danger and potential death as well as a showcase of haunting beauty.

OTHER ANECDOTES

" We are such stuff as dreams are made on;
and our little life is rounded with a sleep."
-Shakespeare-

One fine spring day, I was on routine Gorge patrol and was just turning into the Grays Arch Recreation Area, when a young lady came running towards my vehicle waving her arms. I immediately brought the vehicle to a halt, exited and confronted the lady as to the problem. Thinking the worst, I became alert and scanned the area while she related her dilemma. She had visited the outdoor vault toilet with her cell phone hanging in the back pocket of her jeans. While pulling down her jeans preparing to defecate, the cell phone slipped out of the pocket and down into the unsavory mass of human waste. I was informed the phone had great value to her, and would I please recover it. I was in somewhat of a qualm on how to do this. Then, I remembered the grabber, and I just happened to have one in my vehicle. This tool has movable jaws and is designed for retrieval of cans. However, the toilet vault was relatively deep and the grabber was about 3 feet in length. Careful not to touch the toilet riser, I eased the grabber down to the pungency viscous mixture at the bottom of the vault. Success! The gripper closed over the cell phone, I squeezed it shut and in a brief instant the phone was mine. The lady took the phone in her bare hands, even though it was covered with a slick ooze coating, and began to wipe it clean with toilet paper. My job done, I tried to bow out gracefully. However she extended her hand to me right from the mucilaginous coating on the cell phone and said. "Thank you so much for what you did. I would like to know your name and shake your hand." I gave her my name, but needless to say, I did not take the offered hand. For an instant I recalled a time before when I did not take the offered hand of a dying young lady who seriously needed the contact. However, I decided this was an entirely different circumstance. Satisfied, I resumed patrol leaving the young lady wiping her cell phone.

At the edge of dark one rare summer evening I was called to Koomer Ridge Campground in reference to a missing child. Arriving at the area, I was briefed that a 8 year old child had wandered away from camp and was nowhere to be found. Full darkness had curtained the land by the time a team was assembled and search plans finished. We set out into the shielded night according to a preplanned arrangement. After searching until midnight with no results, I decided to return to the camp and inform the parents of the negative results and that we would continue the sweep. "That's all right." came the astonishing and unexpected reply. "He was asleep in the tent all the while under a blanket. We found him just after you left." I was perplexed and astonished that no one had bothered to let us know as we continued a ghost search. It was a sadder but wiser man that radioed all search teams to signal 8.

I recall the time a middle age man fell about 40 feet off a cliff while trying to reach his dog who fallen just minutes before. Upon reaching both victims, I placed the man on a backboard. He kept complaining of pain in his backside. Easing him toward his side, I discovered a smashed whiskey bottle in his right rear pocket. I spent some 10 minutes in removing fragments of glass from his buttocks before I was able to make the raise. The dog turned out all right.

One rainy night on Red River near Moonshiner's Arch, I was in the process of removing a young man from a ledge, when his companion who was on top of the cliff, leaned over to yell something. He never completed his message. The next thing I knew, an object came hurling by me and landed with a thump at ground level. Startled, I rappelled down and examined the young man who opened his eyes and said, "Hi" before passing out. Miraculous, his injuries were not too serious, but I now had two victims on my hands instead of one. All in a night's work!

A lady was hiking with her dog around the cliffs near Sky Bridge. Her dog bounding ahead slipped and fell over a 30 foot cliff. The lady, while trying to grab the dog plunged over herself. Upon my arrival, the first words the lady said was, "Please take my dog first." Both were injured.

In all my years of service, I never believed that anything could survive a fall from the cliffs of Devil's Canyon. Not only did a dog fall from this overlook, but actually come through with minor injuries. A young man and his girlfriend, along with a dog that was reminiscence of Spuds McKenzie visited the overlook. The dog was not leashed and ran full speed down the trail, continued through the overlook safety fence and plunged over the cliff. I met the frantic young couple on the way out to seek help, and we returned to the overlook. I knew a ledge was about 100 feet down and I hoped the dog had landed there. Otherwise, there was no hope. The drop continued for another 150 feet. Moving to an area of the cliff with the least height, I donned my rappelling gear and over I went. When the ledge was reached, the dog came dragging up to meet me. I could not believe the dog was actually walking, but also did not appear to have a major injury. Moving him to a more sloping part of the cliff wall, I placed him in a dog harness (I had came prepared) and told the people on top to pull him up at my signal. They complied and the dog helped by digging his feet onto the cliff. When he topped the rim, his owners gathered him up and rushed for their car without a backward glance. Certainty, I appreciated their gratitude and concern for my safety. Just bantering. I learned a long time ago if you want thanks, you are in the wrong line of work.

One late fall evening I was involved in a rescue near Parched Corn Creek. I dropped a carabiner into the leaf littered fissured ledge and as I reached down for it I saw a copperhead just inches from my hand. The serpent appeared alert and ready for anything. I slowly withdrew my hand careful to make no sudden move. The snake watched with glistening eyes but made no move to strike or lunge. As I stood up the reptile began to slither away. One of the team members spotted the snake and immediately started to kill it. "Let it go," I admonished, "He let me go." The snake twisted along its sinuous way, and I returned to the rescue at hand. As for me, I was thankful the snake did not strike. As for the snake, he never knew his life had been spared. A brief encounter between a man and a snake on a superb fall evening. The rescue was completed and the victim lived to tell his story, as I am telling mine.

By now the reader is probably wondering what snakes have to do with the sociology of search and rescue. Simply this: Most rescuers see few snakebites in the span of their careers; likewise physicians and nurses. As a result, many rescue people are a little hazy on emergency protocols for venomous bites.

Most people do not treat snakes kindly and many make an effort to kill everyone they see. It would appear that snakes are feared because of dislike of them. The fear of snakes (Ophidiophoba) is one of the most common frights which plague humans.

A young man had fallen from a 50 foot cliff along with his dog. The dog had gone over first and the man followed by trying to seize the dog. When the rescue team arrived, it was decided to lower the victim from the shelf he was on to the bottom of the cliff at distance of only 30 feet. The young man had a broken leg and multiple bruises and contusions. The dog appeared uninjured. Placing the victim in the litter and preparing the necessary ropes and equipment moved swiftly. There was some discussion about how to move the dog, and it was decided that once we got his master on the ground, we would send back the litter for him. The dog was having none of this, since he had already made up his mind. As I guided the litter over the mantle rim, a streak of fur went past me and jumped into the litter, startling the team members doing the lower. As the dog sat quietly with his master the stretcher was slowly and carefully maneuvered to the ground, whereupon the dog jumped out with a joyful bark as if to say, "That was fun. Let's do it again."

A climber fell about 60 feet when his protection pulled out. He had a grievous injury of an almost torn off ankle banging by a few strands of ligaments. The blood vessels had retracted and sealed off so there was very little bleeding. By some prodigy, the doctors were able to reattach his ankle so well that he is active today with only a slight limp.

On the darker side:

Man dies after losing control of an Australian Rappel.
Lady dies in fall from Sky Bridge.
Child drowns in Red River
Youth dies after losing control of a rappel.
Young lady dies of exposure.
Man hangs himself.
Lady commits suicide
Young man falls to his death while trying to jump across crack at Chimney Rock Young lady urinates over edge of cliff and falls to

her death
Young man dies while trying to stop female from falling over cliff.
And 60 others not mentioned.

In a way this missive has wandered back and forth from sociology to how to pluck people from high cliff walls. The Red River Gorge rescue crew is the best possible response to the rescue situation here and does a terrific job. The problem is that such a big job needs to be done at all.

SNAKE ANECDOTES

""We have scotched the snake, not killed it"
-Shakespeare

No analysis of SAR missions would be complete without mention of snake hazards in the terrain of which most rescues occur. There are many varieties of snakes in the Red River Gorge, but most are harmless. Two species of pit vipers can cause a rescuer some concern. They are the Timber Rattlesnake and the Copperhead. It is not my intention to imply these snakes are vicious and just waiting to strike. If fact, they are usually very shy and retiring. When you invade their domain, or unintentionally tread on one--and the snake cannot be expected to know that it was done accidental-- they cast aside this cloak of shyness and step forward a valorous and dangerous warrior. While I am not about speak out on the sociology of snakes, I do want to mention a few veritable anecdotes of snake experiences.

One hot July day, I was going up the north face of Tower Rock to assist a climber who had gotten himself into difficulties at the vertical layback of this climb. Surmounting the first mantle, I found myself face to face with a timber rattler. True to his nature, even though I was somewhat encroaching on his realm, he remained quiet hoping to escape detection. Not to worry! There was no place to go but down and I forthwith beat a hasty retreat. There were other routes to the layback. Mr. Rattler could remain secure in his, and I would seek mine elsewhere.

A young man fell about 50 feet from a cliff. As he was being treated by rescue team members, a copperhead snake crawled from underneath the victim. He must have fallen directly on top of the snake. A good example of the characteristic of this reptile to rarely evince a desire to seek trouble. The snake slithered away as anxious to be gone as we were to have it go.

On another rescue off Pinch-Em-Tight Gap we were carrying out a victim across the most copperhead infested area that I have ever encountered. It was a hot sultry night and these reptiles were slithering everywhere. I heard an oath from one of the friends of the victim, and a thrashing about sound. I played my light in his direction and found he was trying to kick off a copperhead that had attached itself to the rim of his boot. He was ultimately successful. The copperhead went flying and each and every one of us became more acutely aware of our surroundings. We finally made it out without further incident.

I was called to the Slade Rest Area in response to a request to remove a snake from the car of a frantic young lady who had no desire for the companionship of a serpent. I located the snake and removed a harmless ring-necked. How the culprit got into the car is a mystery, however the lady been on Tunnel Ridge previously with her car doors open. This was one of those rare times where the victim was deeply appreciative. I returned the snake to Tunnel Ridge and his freedom.

SNAKEBITE

Records of reported snakebites over the years totaled fifteen bites (Copperhead). There were no reported Rattlesnake bites in the Red River Gorge. This lends credence to the belief that these reptiles are shy and retiring and would much prefer their solitude to an encounter with humans. Given the vast throngs of visitors (many of them shod with sandals or barefoot) it is surprising the bites are so few.

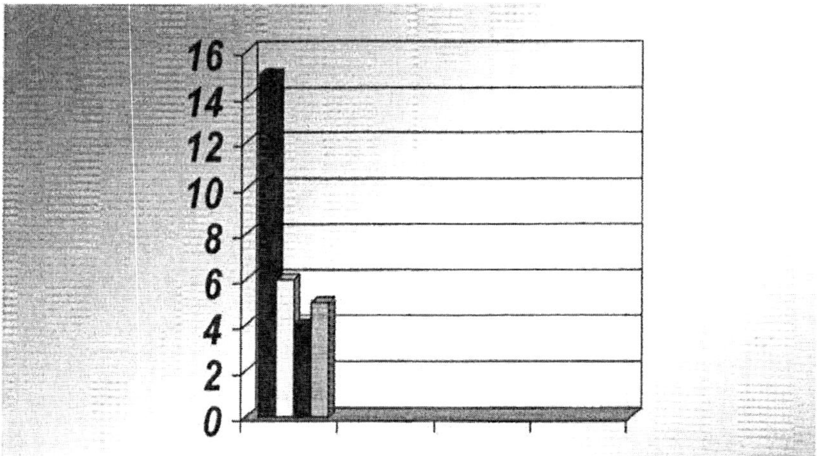

NO. OF BITES	15			
HOSPITAL	6			
CLINIC	4			
UNTREATED	5			

Serpents were mentioned in the biblical account of the Garden of Eden and have suffered a bad reputation since. To the average person snakes

are malign creatures, and the fear of snakes (Ophidiophoba) is one of the most common frights which plague humans

Snakes have the reputation as a doer of evil deeds when they actually assist humans greatly in controlling rodent and insect pests. Most Kentucky snakes are harmless to man. The bite of a copperhead is rarely fatal. The venom, as a general rule, will not kill a healthy adult. Severity of the bite is dependent upon several factors: How much venom was injected. If the snake had just injected into a small animal, the venom sacs would be nearly empty and the human would receive a "Dry Bite". The angle of the hit, and whether the spot was protected with clothing or leather. Nevertheless, the danger of snakebite should not be underestimated

The brown pattern of the copperhead's skin blends almost indiscernibly into a background of dry leaves. Many people coming upon the copperhead may not even see the reptile which ignores all tradition and glides discreetly away. To identify a young copperhead is easy. During the early part of their lives they have a bright yellow tip on their tail, which attracts inquisitive creatures. An ingenious hunting device!

Rattlesnakes are another story. It may be hard to think of the "rattler" as a shrinking violet, yet this notorious reptile is shy and retiring. Rattlers rarely strike when unprovoked and even when encroached upon, they lie quiet hoping to escape detection. They usually strike from an S-shaped position which enables the snake to hit for a distance sometimes exceeding half its length. Rattlesnake bites have been fatal in only about fifteen per cent of all cases not properly treated.

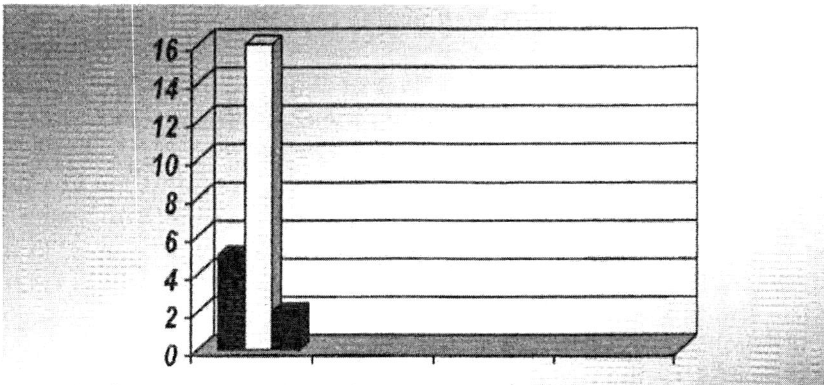

■ DRY BITES	5			
□ NEAR MISS	16			
■ BITE DEFLECTED	2			

The preceding anecdotes were included for a specific purpose: To explain by example the sometimes humorous sociological relationship between rescuer and victim. Rescue is the reiteration of social ties when done by volunteers in an area that calls for a sense of community involvement. However, a new approach to SAR problems may be one which stresses techniques and a commitment to finding the answers to all of one's own exigency, rather than calling for assistance. We need to encourage self-reliance as an individual as a step toward reducing the number of accidents. Tragically many of these situations were not true accidents. Investigation indicated a step-by-step plan which led to emergency. If any one of the many links of that accident chain had been broken, the mishap would not have occurred.

Out of over 1600 SAR missions. I have had the unpleasant job of positioning over 70 dead humans into black plastic body bags. Death accounts for only about 5 % of the total SAR incidents and that's not too bad you say? Statistical, maybe it's not so bad. But compassionate, and especially to relatives it has been a huge impact on their lives.

I vividly recollect the rescue of a young man from a cliff near Sky Bridge. He had fallen over 100 feet and was DOA of the rescue team. I was out of commercial body bags at this time, but did have an army issue one. These consist of a large black plastic sack reminiscent of an oversize refuse bag. and an outer shell of OD nylon. To use it is necessary to fold the plastic bag about half-way down, insert the victim feet first and then folding the bag up and over the head, before placing in the OD nylon shell. As I was following this procedure, with the assistance of one of the team members, I heard him mutter something to the effect that this was "Like stuffing a hog down in a sack!" However this was very early in his SAR career and his outlook has become more empathetic.

It is not the expectation of this writing to integrally point out that SAR may be exhilarating and admirable. The field activities usually are, but the emphasis should he on the SAR event that did not take place. The best SAR event never occurs - it is only heard as a story around the campfire or in the local hangout after an epic on the precipitous cliffs that ultimately turned out fine without injury.

Through the diligent use of PSAR to prevent and minimize as many dangerous situations as possible with the ample use of education and signs. it is conceivable to prognosticate the rescue team sitting around with nothing to do but play chess and dwell on the past rescues of long ago. Shades of the Maytag repairman.

When that day comes!

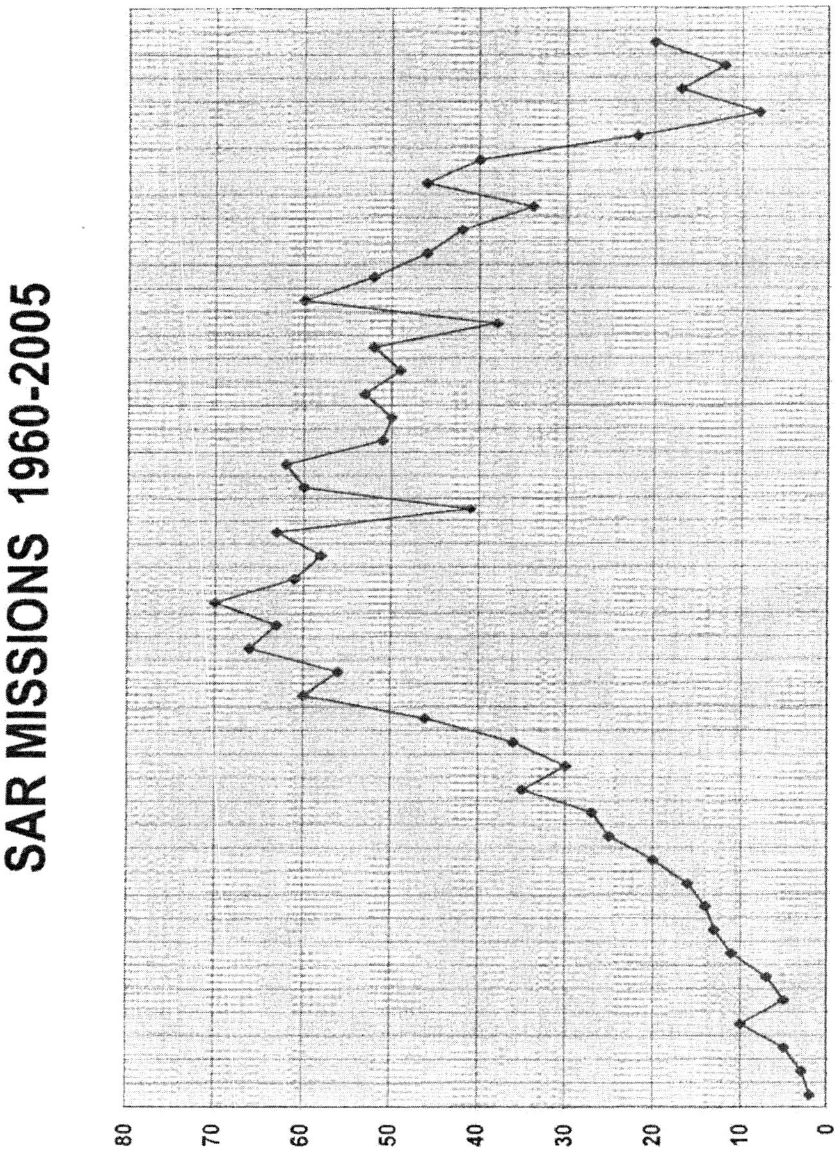
SAR MISSIONS 1960-2005
80
70
60
50
40
30
20
10
0

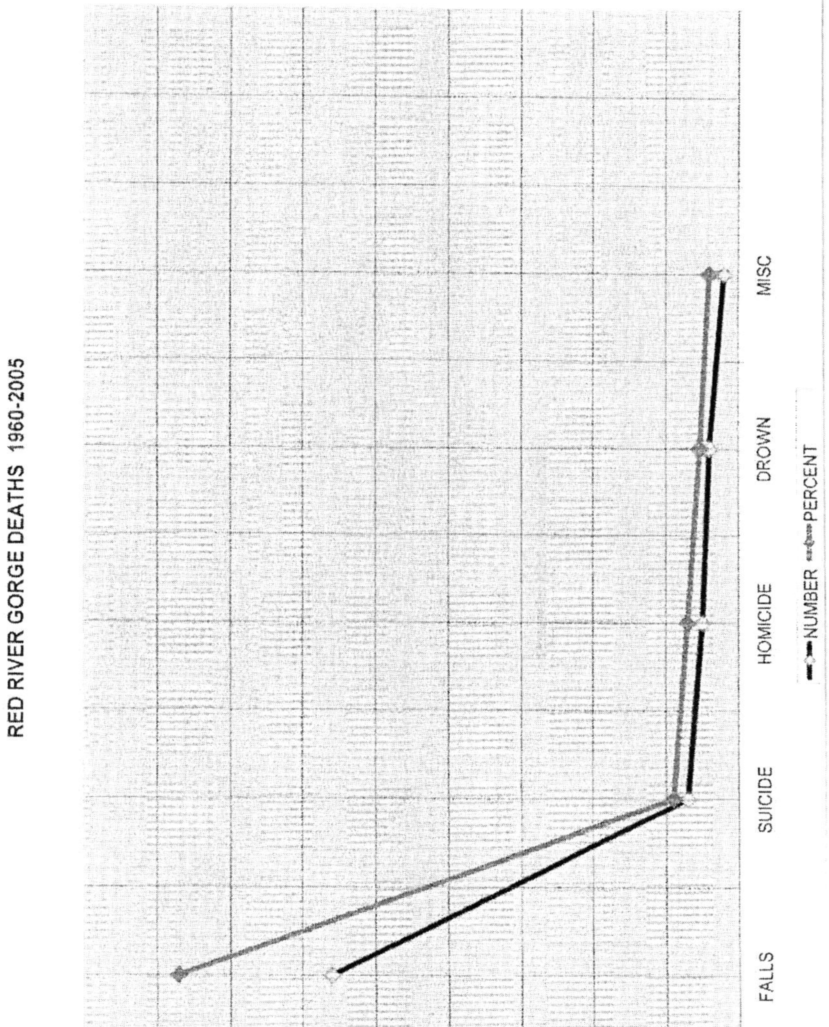
RED RIVER GORGE DEATHS 1960-2005
90
80
70
60
50
40
30
20
10
0
FALLS
SUICIDE
HOMICIDE
DROWN
MISC
NUMBER
PERCENT

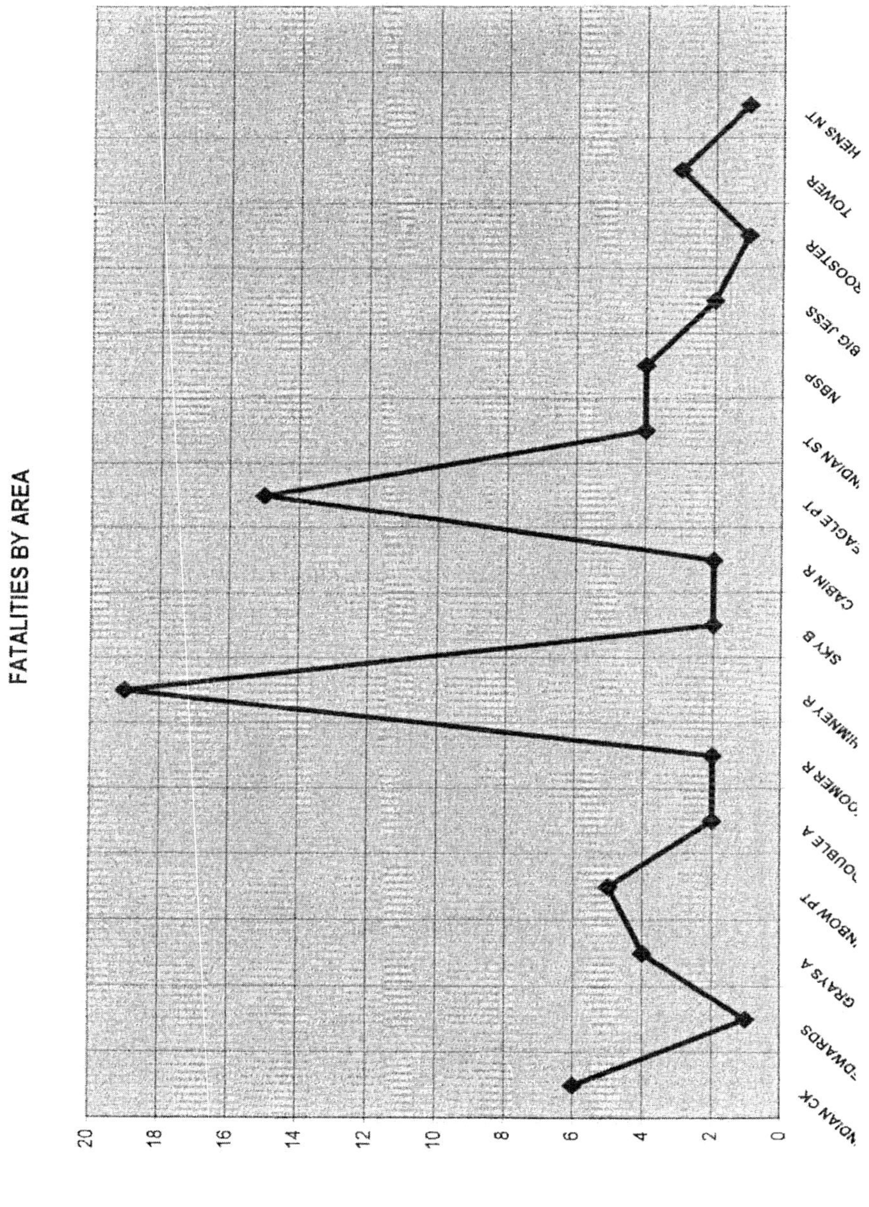

FATALITIES BY AREA
20
18
16
14
12
10
8
6
4
2
0
NDIAN CK
DWARDS
GRAYS A
NBOW PT
OUBLE A
OOMER R
HIMNEY R
SKY B
CABIN R
AGLE PT
NDIAN ST
NBSP
BIG JESS
OOSTER
TOWER
HENS NT

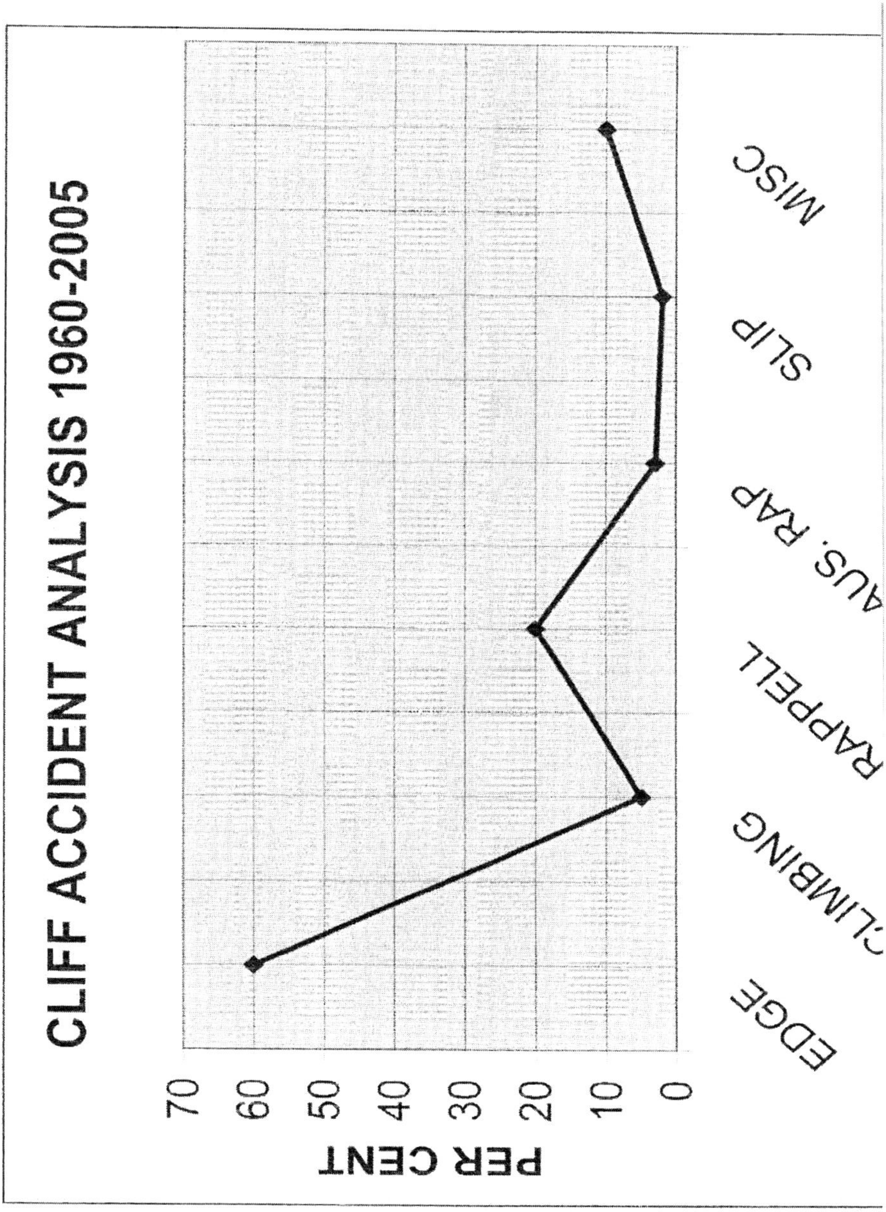

CLIFF ACCIDENT ANALYSIS 1960-2005
PER CENT
70
60
50
40
30
20
10
0
EDGE
CLIMBING
RAPPELL
AUS. RAP
SLIP
MISC

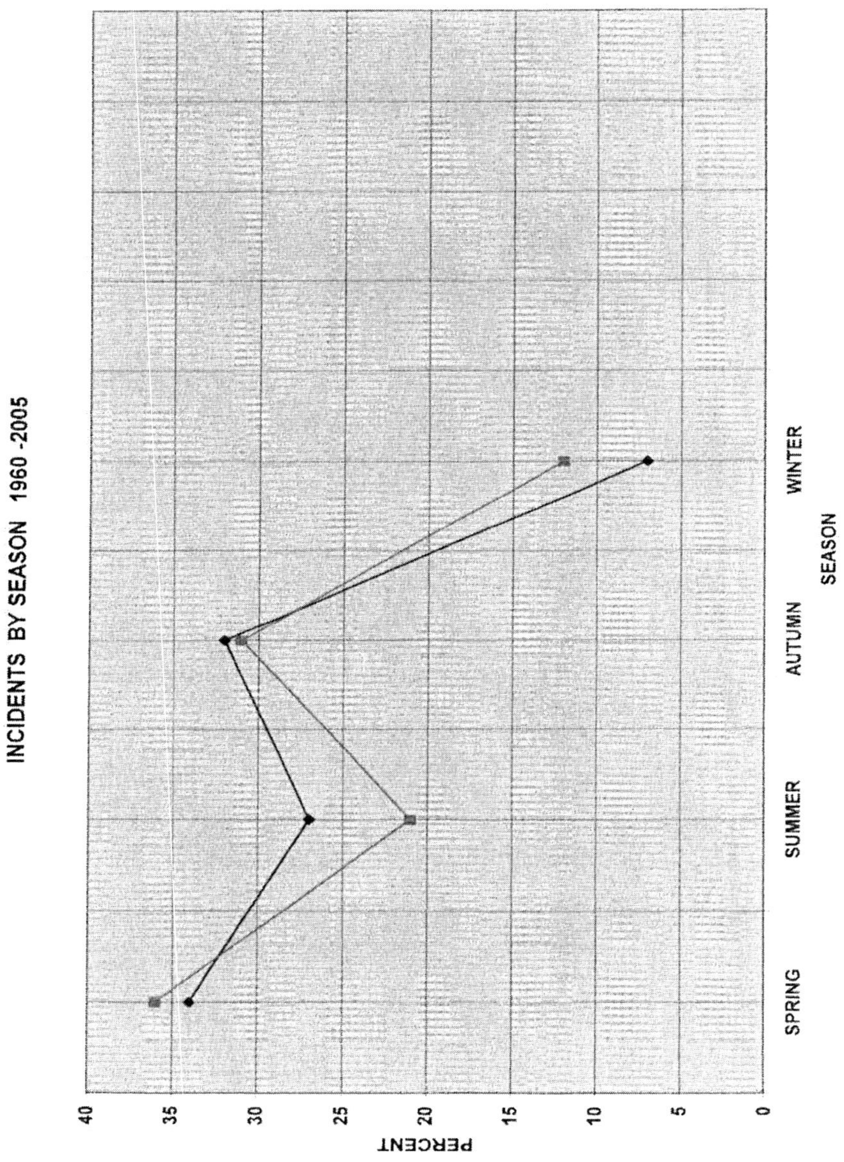

INCIDENTS BY SEASON 1960 -2005
PERCENT
0
5
10
15
20
25
30
35
40
SPRING
SUMMER
AUTUMN
WINTER
SEASON

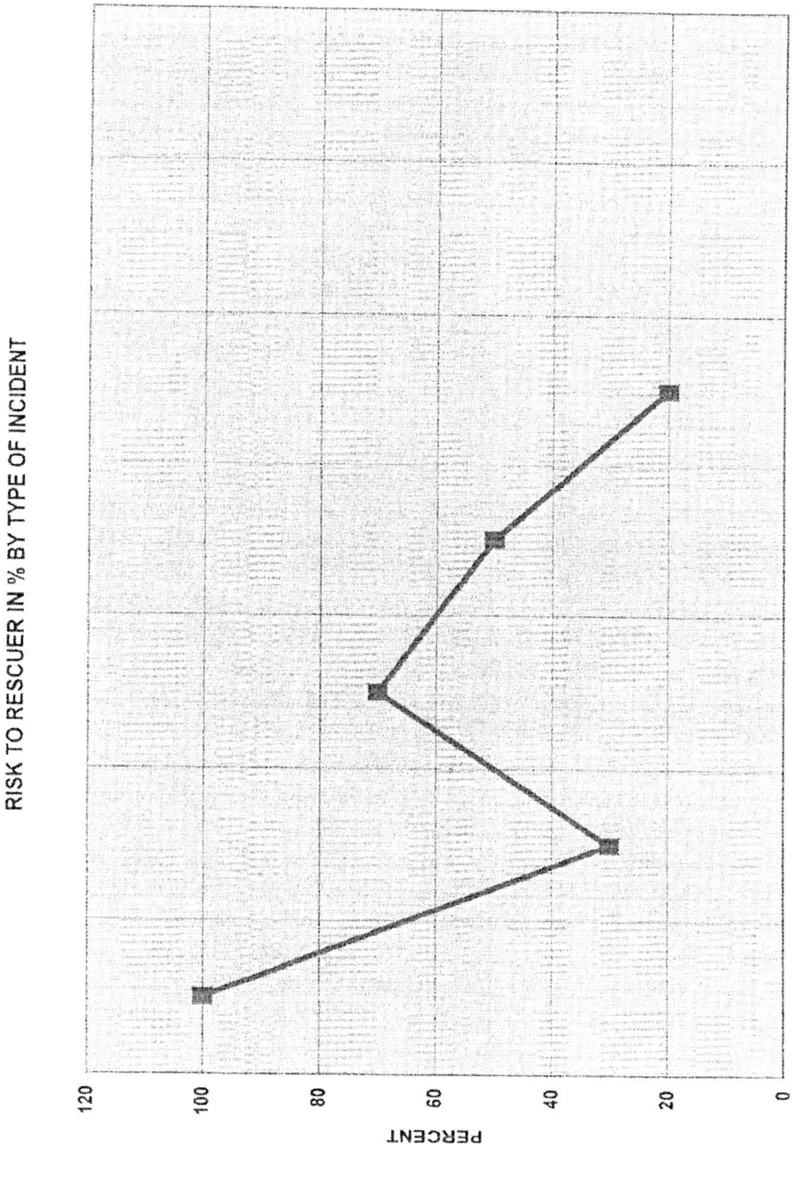
RISK TO RESCUER IN % BY TYPE OF INCIDENT
PERCENT
120
100
80
60
40
20
0

INCIDENTS BY GENDER 1960-2005

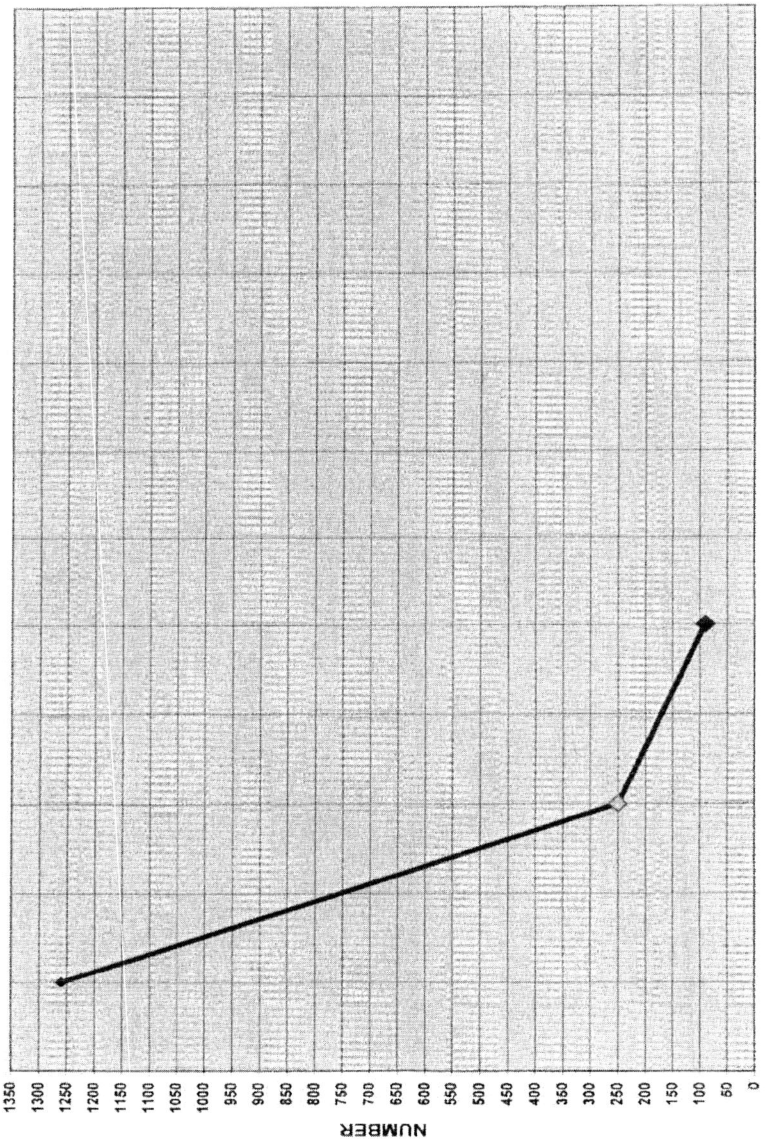

The preceding graphs chronicle 45 years of search and rescue in the Red River Gorge and over 1600 missions.

RESCUE SCENES

N305PH

N305PH

THE HANGING AT INDIAN CREEK

It was a superb late autumn evening as I was returning to the Gorge after a day in Federal Court. The falling leaves were swirling and dancing off my windshield as I was thinking how pleasant the day. I was preoccupied with this thought and failed to decipher the radio traffic. Better check in just in case. The voice of the dispatcher was clear now, while informing me of a report of a person hanging from a bridge, an apparent suicide by hanging. My mood shifted gears as I turned for Indian Creek.

Arriving at the Bridge on Road 9B, I dismounted and scanned the bridge. Noting a thin white nylon rope tied to the railing, I leaned over and observed a fairly young white male hanging by the neck with the white rope. I observed for any indications of life and decided to rappel down to the subject for a closer look. Descending to where I was level with him, I checked the subject even as the edge of dark moved over his face. Finding no signs of life, I returned to my vehicle and notified dispatch while awaiting the coming of the coroner. Darkness had shrouded the land when he arrived.

After consultation, and at the request of coroner, I started the process of a body recovery. Attaching ropes to the bridge rails, I again rappelled to the body and secured with ropes. Warning those on top there would be a sudden weight on the ropes, I whipped out my buck knife. It was the work of an instant to slice through the thin nylon rope and lower the body to the stream bed. I continued my rappel to the bottom, where I was joined by the coroner. After his examination, we placed the subject in a body bag and carried to the vehicle

The subject had a suicide note attached which spoke to depression, family problems and debts. It is so final when the bag is zipped shut and what was once a fellow human is now a faceless entity being rapidly covered by the cascading autumn leaves. It leaves me wondering, given our short lifespan, what depths of despair made him feel this was necessary

Well, as I approach the end of my 45th year of SAR, it is obvious

I have left out many important things from this document Not a word about the car fire killing four people at Chimney Top. The individual who fell almost 150 feet from a cliff and actually walked out, the first rappel from a helicopter and many other events.

It is difficult to abbreviate 45 years into a few pages of paper, but I will shrink a few stories that should be told.

The call was a climber had fallen at Hen's Nest Rock. My mind shifted to logistics, do we approach the rock from Sky Bridge or from the Red River? Learning he was already on the ground, I decided on a river approach. Team members were scarce this day. There were only Dan Doursen and I, however one of the victim's friends assured me there a group of climbers at the rock. The three of us set out with the Stokes Litter for Hen's Nest Rock through intensely rugged terrain.

At Hen's nest we found a climber down with a back injury and several young men willing to act as litter bearers. Preparing the victim for the torturous pack out was accomplished and we were moving toward the river arriving without further incident. Now a decision of whether we should try to cross the river, or follow the bank to the concrete bridge was impending. Crossing the river with a victim is treacherous, but the highway was just on the other side. To follow the riverbank to the concrete bridge was about a mile. I decided to put it to a vote, which turned out a tie. The victim spoke from the stokes in a clear voice, "If I have a vote, lets cross the river." That decided it! Selecting a crossing I knew was fairly shallow, we plunged into the Red with the litter. The crossing was without incident, except the water was deeper than I had anticipated. The victim got a little wet, but was soon in the ambulance enroute to the hospital. A few years later this same individual suffered a heart attack while climbing and died on the way to the hospital.
Then there was the dog that had been stranded on a cliff ledge for several days. So glad to see someone he almost knocked me from the ledge while trying to rescue him. I have learned to carry a dog harness for such incident. It was a happy ending as I returned the dog to its grateful owners.
A daring young teenager set out to do an Australian rappel

from the summitof Eagles Peak, lost control and plunged head first into the rocks below, a body bag case

Another Australian rappel involved too much slack in the rope, breaking a carabiner when the slack played out. Subject fell over 80 feet and eventually recovered to tell his story.

An unknown call for assistance at Sky Bridge. As I came barreling in, I noted a large group of motorcycles and occupants with black leather jackets emblazoned on the back with "Hells Angels", were blocking the road. Too late to back out now, so I boldly asked what was going on. Who wants to know, came the reply. I quickly recognized this situation called for diplomacy and tact. I had observed several cars in the parking lot which appeared to be visitors. I'm Federal Law Enforcement Officer Don Fig, will someone please explain the situation here. Reckon I can, a big burly man spoke up, "You see, we are short on cash and these good people have agreed to pay $10.00 per car if we let them out. Choosing my next words carefully I replied, What you are proposing is illegal and I must ask you to let these people go." "You going to make us", came the testy reply from the burly one, who appeared to be the leader. With every muscle tense I spoke loud and clear, "There are 30 of you and one of me, I don't think I can MAKE you do anything. Something about the humor of the situation must have struck the burley one and he said, 'Fig, I'll never forget that name" and with these words he opened the road . It was highly grateful visitors I waved out of the parking lot.

On a rescue at Indian Stairway I called for a helicopter. The daring and skillful pilot set down the craft right in the middle of the Gladie Creek Bridge! A FIRST in my long career.

Subject was camping on top of a high cliff near Sky Bridge. He was gathering firewood to fuel a campfire. He apparently was momentarily blinded by the flames and stumbled over the edge, falling about 120 feet.

Subject was camped on a pinnacle rock.. During the early morning hours he straddled a large crack in the rock and commenced to defecate. His balance shifted and he fell into the crack.

This could go on and on, example by example and still not accomplish anything more than a study of visitor behavior on the high cliffs. This scenario repeats over and over while relatives visit cemeteries or push wheelchairs.
If I am waxing a bit morbid, it is because I have removed so many young people from the precipitous ledges, scores of them in the stark confines of a body bag. Notwithstanding the quadriplegics and paraplegics as a result of the unforgiving high cliffs.

I failed to mention Charlie Rowe, who has seen his share of rescues in the Gorge. A highly capable young man, who has a special adaptation for rope rigging, responds to incidents when he can. He has the potential to become an outstanding rescuer, possessing the special attributes of attitude, knowledge of Gorge, and espirit de corps. He is an excellent candidate for "Passing The Torch".

Body found in Red River Gorge

Friends join dogged search
For Red River Gorge hiker

The newspaper captions on SAR glare ominously from the page conveying to the reader separate messages to separate individuals

To kindred spirits a message of sorrow, such as What a waste, how sad for the family, what were they doing that caused the accident.

To the general reader perhaps a touch of grief at the death and danger existing in a place that for many is a celebration of life as they are caught up in the next wave

To those whom have never been to the Gorge, a dangerous place-should be closed

To the rescuer a statement of a job well done, but also a message of failure. There is little dignity to death on the high cliffs

Having worked the area for 45+ years I believe the Gorge to be no more intrinsically dangerous than driving a vehicle to get there. Consider this: No dangerous cliffs, only dangerous people

THE LAST HURRAH

"A time to be born and a time to die"
-Ecc-

This epistle chronicles the 45 year (1969 -2005) SAR career of an aging USFS Law Enforcement Officer. From training, accepting the rigors of discipline, to actual rescues learning the price of survival, and the harsh realities of death on the high cliffs. Now with most of a long career history, the ghostly specter of retirement is just over the horizon. .As with anyone dedicated to a purpose, "The last Hurrah" is needed as a final searing entry in this chronicle.

From a practical viewpoint, this is improbable. Knees, hammered against the cliff walls for almost a half-century have finally deteriorated to the point where walking downhill is tortuous. A rappel is difficult and climbing is out of the question. So the probability of the "great rescue" is fading into obscurity, even as I.

But is it, after all, so discordant? It has been a glorious career, in which I have taken great pride, not withstanding working amid some of the most outstanding scenery in the nation. If I had the chance I would do it all over again.

Many people have commented on my luck to have survived all the missions relatively unscathed. Maybe they are right. I guess my "luck" has always been people. People like Ken Munday, Grizzly Cloyd, James Cloyd, Johnny Faulkner, Kenneth Scarberry, Click Castle and always Kendal Culbertson,

Yet, with pride, I remember the Forest service all volunteer rescue team and how for one brief moment in time they were a shining example. Gone now, scattered to the four winds. With Kendal's retirement, the last of a vanishing breed passed into history. What can I say about Kendal Culbertson? His exploits are legendary among the rescue community, and his departure has left a void in the team that cannot be replaced, only succeeded. The unequaled safety record of the team was largely due to his "eagle eye" spotting potential problems before they

became a reality. A most extraordinary individual who admirably served the team for well over a quarter century,_ who still stands reads to respond to an emergency situation where his expertise is needed.

Then, there is Kenneth Scarberry, USFS Law Enforcement Officer, upon whose broad shoulders the burden of command will fall. Who must make authority decisions quickly and accurately, and coordinate the various rescue contingents into one unit. I have every confidence in this fine young man as he enters into this colossal epic arena "So That Others Might Live" and wish for him the highest success in this endeavor.

My steadfast wife, Susie, has endured almost 45 years of Search and Rescue missions, uncomplaining, along with hundreds of late night law enforcement calls. In fact, our younger years found her actively involved in several such events, and her support has been phenomenal. She has, of course, my undying gratitude, not only as a wife, but as an acknowledged peer. She strongly encouraged the writing of Tales of the Red River Gorge, Fitchburg Furnace and this missive. Whatever I am, have been, and yet to be, I owe to this astonishing woman who has been a stalwart companion on life's journey.

November 2004, chronicled my last year as a Federal Law Enforcement Officer. When the missive came through channels, I had exceeded my mandatory retirement age by eleven years. What did LE supervisor Mike Gay do? Did he telephone and bluntly announce I was being retired? No, he had the courtesy to take time for a personal visit to let me know the situation. This thoughtful act greatly reduced the pain of being told you are too old. The point I wish to make is Mike could have taken the telephone route, but he knew this was an important issue with me and I deeply appreciate his concern.

A few days later Captain Dennis Whitehead, along with Forest Supervisor Ben Worthington, came to collect my credentials and defensive gear. This fine thing helped alleviate the sadness such events bring and allowed focus on the accomplishments. This is very special to an old man whose career is winding down.

My thoughts go back to the early days of LE, when agency policy was low key. Things have changed considerable since those days and for the better. It has been my privilege to have worked alongside Kendal

Culbertson and Kenneth Scarberry, amid some of the most spectacular scenery in the nation.

At this writing, I am the Center Director of the new Gladie Cultural and Environmental Learning Center, a building I worked toward for over a quarter century and from where I shall eventually retire. It feels as if I have been put out to pasture, but I am thankful I am still in the environment I love which has given me so much. Someone remarked there were worse pastures and I fully agree. Every day I drive to the Center I am in the midst of spectacular scenery and am renewed

I am presently engaged in training an untried team and even under controlled conditions, the maneuvers required are becoming increasing difficult. Time to admit the job is too tough and turn it over to the young and vigorous.

Ecclesiastes reads, "To everything there is a season." Most appropriate now as a new season is impending. The team is almost ready as I can make them for the monumental task of SAR in the Gorge. I have done all I can do and have a feeling the coming season will be in good hands.

I approach the end of my career with a mixture of trepidation, sorrow, regret and a touch of relief, while at the same time looking forward to following the performance of the new "Keepers of the Gorge."

After 45+ years of SAR, will the late night telephone rings or the sound of sirens raw hiding through the Gorge trigger an automatic response? It is something 1 have always known. There can be only A' Tout a' l' Heure!